January

S	S	M	T	W	T	F
				1	2	3
4	5	6	7	8	9	10
11	12	13	14	15	16	17
18	19	20	21	22	23	24
25	26	27	28	29	30	31

February

S	S	M	T	W	T	F
1	2	3	4	5	6	7
8	9	10	11	12	13	14
15	16	17	18	19	20	21
22	23	24	25	26	27	28

March

S	S	M	T	W	T	F
1	2	3	4	5	6	7
8	9	10	11	12	13	14
15	16	17	18	19	20	21
22	23	24	25	26	27	28
29	30	31				

April

S	S	M	T	W	T	F
			1	2	3	4
5	6	7	8	9	10	11
12	13	14	15	16	17	18
19	20	21	22	23	24	25
26	27	28	29	30		

May

S	S	M	T	W	T	F
31					1	2
3	4	5	6	7	8	9
10	11	12	13	14	15	16
17	18	19	20	21	22	23
24	25	26	27	28	29	30

June

S	S	M	T	W	T	F
	1	2	3	4	5	6
7	8	9	10	11	12	13
14	15	16	17	18	19	20
21	22	23	24	25	26	27
28	29	30				

July

S	S	M	T	W	T	F
			1	2	3	4
5	6	7	8	9	10	11
12	13	14	15	16	17	18
19	20	21	22	23	24	25
26	27	28	29	30	31	

August

S	S	M	T	W	T	F
30	31					1
2	3	4	5	6	7	8
9	10	11	12	13	14	15
16	17	18	19	20	21	22
23	24	25	26	27	28	29

September

S	S	M	T	W	T	F
		1	2	3	4	5
6	7	8	9	10	11	12
13	14	15	16	17	18	19
20	21	22	23	24	25	26
27	28	29	30			

October

S	S	M	T	W	T	F
				1	2	3
4	5	6	7	8	9	10
11	12	13	14	15	16	17
18	19	20	21	22	23	24
25	26	27	28	29	30	31

November

S	S	M	T	W	T	F
1	2	3	4	5	6	7
8	9	10	11	12	13	14
15	16	17	18	19	20	21
22	23	24	25	26	27	28
29	30					

December

S	S	M	T	W	T	F
		1	2	3	4	5
6	7	8	9	10	11	12
13	14	15	16	17	18	19
20	21	22	23	24	25	26
27	28	29	30	31		

A YEAR IN 120 RECIPES

Jack Monroe

PHOTOGRAPHY BY SUSAN BELL

MICHAEL JOSEPH
an imprint of
PENGUIN BOOKS

Penguin
Random
House

MICHAEL JOSEPH

Published by the Penguin Group

Penguin Books Ltd, 80 Strand, London WC2R 0RL, England

Penguin Group (USA) Inc., 375 Hudson Street, New York, New York 10014, USA

Penguin Group (Canada), 90 Eglinton Avenue East, Suite 700, Toronto, Ontario,
Canada M4P 2Y3 (a division of Pearson Penguin Canada Inc.)

Penguin Ireland, 25 St Stephen's Green, Dublin 2, Ireland (a division of Penguin Books Ltd)

Penguin Group (Australia), 707 Collins Street, Melbourne, Victoria 3008, Australia
(a division of Pearson Australia Group Pty Ltd)

Penguin Books India Pvt Ltd, 11 Community Centre,
Panchsheel Park, New Delhi – 110 017, India

Penguin Group (NZ), 67 Apollo Drive, Rosedale, Auckland 0632,
New Zealand (a division of Pearson New Zealand Ltd)

Penguin Books (South Africa) (Pty) Ltd, Block D, Rosebank Office Park,
181 Jan Smuts Avenue, Parktown North, Gauteng 2193, South Africa

Penguin Books Ltd, Registered Offices: 80 Strand, London WC2R 0RL, England

www.penguin.com

First published 2014
001

Set in Esfera NF and Helvetica Neue
Colour reproduction by Altaimage, London
Printed and bound in Italy by Printer Trento srl

A CIP catalogue record for this book is available from the British Library

ISBN: 978—0—718—17996—0

Contents

Introduction

To my one –
One cannot eat well, write well, dine well, if one has not loved well. Or something.
So thank you, for a pretty good year.

It's been a pretty good year. A pretty good, if extraordinary, year. That's what I keep telling myself, and various other people who ask me how I'm doing. Old friends, new friends, journalists and inquisitive strangers, all trying to piece together the blanks in the ten-pounds-a-week-food-shop girl to number-one-bestselling-author story. Well, I shrug, I couldn't have planned and executed it if I'd tried.

In my previous (and first) book, *A Girl Called Jack,* I signed off the epilogue with a diary entry from my blog from July 2013: 'Hunger Hurts – One Year Later'. It's as true today for half a million families in the UK as it was for me, typing through angry tears on 30 July last year, that poverty isn't just having no heating, or not quite enough food, or unplugging your fridge and turning your hot water off. Poverty is the sinking feeling when Small Boy finishes his one Weetabix and says, 'More, Mummy? Bread and jam, please, Mummy,' as you're trying to work out how to carry the TV and the guitar to the pawn shop, and how to tell him that there is no bread and jam.

Since that entry, I've handed in and published my first book, appeared on the front cover of *Observer Food Monthly* (looking fierce with a rolling pin), sworn at a senior politician very emphatically on prime-time television, was the face of a Sainsbury's campaign, laughed my way through a stonking hangover on *The Wright Stuff,* and moved house, doubling the size of my family to two grown women, two small children, two cats, two guinea pigs and three very special fish. I wept when one guinea pig died, RIP Dibble, and moved the surviving one on to the kitchen table, where he is dearly loved, spoilt to bits and an excellent receptacle for withered vegetables, peelings and the children's porridge when they aren't looking.

And through it all, I've cooked, baked, created, stirred, scrabbled around in the fridge and rustled up dinner after dinner after dinner. I've been on holiday – REAL HOLIDAY – something I hadn't done in a very long time! Thanks to the success of my first book, and that's a thanks to every single one of you who bought a copy, and my weekly *Guardian* column, I finally feel as though, after almost three years, I have my feet on some sort of level ground again.

So, to answer the oft-asked question: no, I'm no longer living on a food budget of ten pounds a week. For a start, there's twice as many people to feed these days, so although I can do it for two of us over five days during the annual Live Below the Line challenge to raise money for Oxfam, it's not the weekly shopping total any more. But in those days I learned to cook and eat well without spending an awful lot of money, and I still stick to those principles. I rinse my baked beans, keep a few frozen green veg on

hand, use value pasta and rice for everything, and get through several cans of chopped tomatoes and other tinned staples a week. Good food doesn't have to cost the earth – and it's definitely not all *foie gras* and caviar at my place. (I'd rather have a flash-fried chicken liver or some creamy herring roe anyway.)

I've divided this book in a roughly seasonal way to guide you through the year, with some personal anecdotes peppered (and salted) throughout. You can buy your fruit and veg from the supermarket, farmers' market or greengrocer, or get it delivered (check out www.abelandcole.co.uk for a fab selection of fruit and veg boxes that magically turn up on your doorstep!). Do whatever's right for you. We're pretty lucky in the UK in that most fruit and vegetables are available most of the year, but if you buy in season, you'll get the best-tasting, most succulent fruit and veg for a fraction of the price you'll pay for the rest of the year. But cook what you like when you like: I'm not policing your cauliflower in April or your tomatoes at Christmas.

I still grow my herbs: I have coriander, mint, parsley, thyme and basil, and a little chilli plant. I've added fennel to my spice collection, on top of turmeric, paprika and cumin, because I received an enormous bag of it from a reader and have used it liberally since. It's available fairly cheaply from ethnic grocery stores or your local supermarket.

Most importantly, use this book as a rough guide: I only ever get the scales out for baking, and weigh everything else with my eyes and instincts. Honestly, you can't go far wrong with a few extra grams of pasta here and there or a different type of green vegetable. Think of my recipes as suggestions, and adapt them to use what you have and what you like. I won't be offended if you tweak them a bit – honest! Write all over this book, cover it with Post-it notes and your own annotations. In my household the food books I love are defaced, spines bent from heavy use and covered with oil, smears of spices, splatters of red sauce and crusty dollops of dough. Get it out, use it, love it, make it your own. Or ours, if you like.

With love,

Jack xxx

JUL|AUG
01

beetroot | green beans | garlic
tomatoes | peaches | courgettes

And here we begin where *A Girl Called Jack* left off: with me sleeping on the floor on a single mattress in a house I shared with five other people. I shared my bedroom with my son. The house was beautiful – clean and bright with friendly lodgers and a huge kitchen – but I ate, washed and slept in one room and became something of a recluse, popping out a few times a week to tend the herbs in the herb garden. I was working as a reporter for my local newspaper, the *Southend Echo* – they had taken me on with no qualifications, apart from a handful of GCSEs, and no experience, apart from perching in the public gallery at local council meetings and writing about them on my blog. It's not all doom and gloom, however – these sunny summer months are glorious for cheap and cheerful fruit and veg, such as bright pink beetroot, green beans, plump red tomatoes and abundant courgettes ...

Roast beetroot and cheese pasta

Beetroot is a great natural food colouring. If you use fresh ones, keep the peelings and put them in a bag in the freezer to save them for later, then pop them into a pan of pasta water or a risotto to turn it pink! Great for kids' parties, or just because – well, who wouldn't fancy a bowl of Barbie-pink risotto every now and again? The eagle-eyed among you will have spotted that this is a pasta recipe, not a risotto – unlike me to get distracted . . .

Serves 2

250g beetroot, fresh or vacuum-packed

2 tablespoons oil, sunflower or groundnut

1 tablespoon runny honey

a pinch of salt

a pinch of dried chilli flakes

1 onion

150g spaghetti or penne pasta

100g soft cream cheese

100g hard, strong cheese

Preheat the oven to 180°C/350°F/gas 4.

Peel and cut the beetroot into small chunks. Place in a roasting dish or, to cook on the hob, in a shallow non-stick pan. Mix together the oil and honey, add a pinch of salt and the chilli flakes, stir and pour over the beetroot. Peel and cut the onion into larger chunks. Add it to the dish, or pan, and stir everything together to distribute the oil and honey mixture evenly. Roast for 40 minutes until the beetroot is soft and the edges charred. (If you are using vacuum-packed beetroot, reduce the cooking time by half.) If cooking on the hob, sauté over a medium heat for around 20 minutes.

Meanwhile, bring a pan of water to the boil and cook the pasta according to the packet instructions, usually around 8–10 minutes.

When the veg is ready, tip it into a blender with any residual honey and oil. Add the cream cheese and a tablespoon or two of the pasta cooking water to loosen, then blitz to an amazingly bright pink purée. Grate the hard, strong cheese.

Drain and rinse the pasta, then toss the sauce through it.

To serve, top with the grated cheese.

Oat-battered kippers with beetroot mash

Growing up beside the sea makes battered fish a rite of passage from my childhood, as far back as I can remember. Here is my grown-up take on it for a speedy supper. I've left the crunchy coating plain, but chilli or black pepper will add a bit of heat, or scatter in some finely chopped parsley for a light, fresh flavour.

Serves 2

2 beetroot

500g potatoes

2 rounded tablespoons plain flour

100ml milk

30g porridge oats

2 kipper fillets

50g butter, plus extra for the mash (optional)

a fistful of flat-leaf parsley

1 lemon, cut into wedges

Peel and dice the beetroot and the potatoes. Bring a large pan of water to the boil, put them in and simmer until tender, for 12–15 minutes.

Meanwhile, make the batter: stir the flour and milk together with two-thirds of the oats. The mixture should be thick but workable.

Place the kipper fillets skin-side down on a board and spread the batter on to the flesh, right to the edges. Scatter the remaining oats over the top.

Heat the butter in a frying pan over a medium–high heat. Place the kippers in the pan batter-side down and fry for 5 minutes, using a spatula to press them down so they cook evenly, until golden and crisp. Carefully turn over and cook for 1 minute on the skin side to crisp.

Chop enough parsley to fill a tablespoon. Drain the beetroot and potatoes, then mash with the parsley and a little butter, if you like. Serve with the kippers, the lemon, and vegetables of your choice.

TIP: Kippers have a lot of tiny pin-bones, so if they don't appeal, try another strong smoked fish, like haddock, instead. I use those 'boil in the bag' kippers that come ready smoked with a little knob of butter – but use whatever's available to you. A kipper is a kipper is a kipper.

Beetroot, feta cheese and lentil salad

I use pre-cooked beetroot in this dish as the vacuum packs are often cheaper than buying fresh. Vacuum-packed beetroot are also quicker to prepare and cook. If you have fresh beetroot, simply peel, dice and cook it in oil for 10 minutes over a medium heat before adding the onion.

Serves 2

125g pre-cooked beetroot

1 onion

1 tablespoon oil, sunflower or groundnut

300ml water

100g red lentils

salt and pepper

a sprig of mint

130g spinach, lamb's lettuce, watercress or salad leaves

50g feta cheese

Dice the beetroot into 1cm chunks. Peel and finely chop the onion. Warm the oil in a frying pan over a medium heat, then add the beetroot and onion. Cook for 8–10 minutes until they soften.

Boil the water. Rinse the lentils, add to the onion and beetroot with 100ml of the water and stir well.

When the liquid has absorbed, add another 100ml of the water and keep stirring to prevent sticking. Repeat until the lentils have softened but are still al dente. Taste, and season.

Strip the mint leaves off the stalk and chop them.

Put the beetroot mixture on a bed of leaves – spinach, lamb's lettuce, watercress or mixed leaves work well – and crumble over the feta cheese. Scatter the mint across the top and serve.

TIPS: If you like a dressing with your salad, mix a squeeze of lemon juice with a tablespoon of oil and a splash of red or white wine vinegar, then drizzle liberally over the top.

This dish also works well with brown or Puy lentils, or plain white rice in place of the red lentils.

Parmesan-crumbed chicken livers with a self-dressing beetroot and mandarin salad   Serves 2

My favourite way to eat chicken livers is flash-fried and tossed in a big juicy salad – in fact, just like this. The sweet fresh flavour of the mandarin perfectly complements the strong taste of liver, and as far as salads go, this one is fairly effortless. If you think it isn't for you, I cooked this for two film colleagues at the *Guardian*, who claimed they didn't like liver, and both ate this with gusto. Liver is extremely inexpensive, packed with iron and vitamins. And it's totally yummy, or it wouldn't be in this book. I rest my case. You're either convinced or you're not!

300g chicken livers • 40g hard, strong cheese • 1 egg • 1 rounded tablespoon flour • a splash of oil, sunflower or groundnut, to fry

For the salad: 1 beetroot, pre-cooked or raw • 1 x 200g tin of mandarins • a few fistfuls of spinach • a splash of oil, sunflower or groundnut • salt and pepper

Rinse your chicken livers under the cold tap, then drain. Cut out any green bits and set to one side.

Now make the salad. If you're using pre-cooked beetroot, dice it into 1cm pieces. If you're using fresh beetroot, peel and grate it finely. Briefly rinse the chopped or grated beetroot under a cold tap in a colander or sieve to get rid of the excess purple juices, and set it to one side. Drain the mandarins, reserving the juice.

Pop the spinach into a salad bowl, add the beetroot and mandarins, and toss with the splash of oil and a few tablespoons of mandarin juice. Toss again for good measure, and pop into the fridge while you cook the chicken livers.

Prepare your liver station. Grate the cheese. Break the egg into a bowl and beat it. In a separate bowl, mix together the flour and grated cheese. Half fill a third bowl with warm water, and fold a tea-towel next to it – you'll need this: you're about to get messy.

Heat a splash of oil in a frying pan over a medium heat. Take one liver, pat it into the flour and cheese mixture, shake off the excess, dunk it in the egg, shake off the excess, roll it back in the flour and cheese mixture, and pop it into the frying pan for 5 minutes, until the cheesy outside is crisp. Repeat until all the livers are done, intermittently dipping your fingers into the water bowl and drying them with the tea-towel as you go. You might need to do these in batches, in which case, remove the cooked livers and keep them warm on a plate or a piece of kitchen paper while you continue with the rest.

To serve, divide the salad between 2 plates and place the livers on top. And enjoy!

Turkey and chickpea burgers

This recipe makes a LOT of burgers. I use the chickpeas to pad them out and make them cheaper, and fling any leftovers on to a baking tray to open-freeze, bagging them up 24 hours later. They're a handy standby for barbecue season, or for those evenings when you don't fancy cooking from scratch. I used to make them for myself when I was working out a lot (a long time ago!) as they're packed with protein too.

Makes 8–10 burgers

400g chickpeas or any white beans

400g turkey mince

1 rounded teaspoon cumin or other spice, or herb, of your choice

2 rounded tablespoons flour

salt and pepper

a splash of oil, sunflower or groundnut, for frying

beetroot, to serve

To make the burgers, drain the chickpeas or beans and mash them well to form a purée. You may need to add a tablespoon of water, but bear in mind that any extra liquid added might mean extra flour is needed at the end to hold them together.

Break up the mince with your hands and mix it into the bean mash well. Stir in the cumin, or whichever spice or herb you've chosen, and the flour, and season well with salt and pepper. Cover the mixture with cling film or a plate, and pop in the fridge for 30 minutes to firm up. (If you don't have time for this, crack an egg into the burger mixture to bind it together, with an extra tablespoon of flour, and stir well.)

Shape the burger mix into 8–10 decent-sized patties – don't worry if you have a small family: they will keep in the fridge for 2 days or in the freezer for up to 3 months.

Heat the splash of oil in a frying pan, and cook the burgers over a medium heat for 8 minutes on each side, turning once.

Serve with a few slices of beetroot balanced on top of each burger.

TIP: If you have any fresh beetroot kicking about, grate it into the chickpea and mince mixture to make your burgers go even further – and go pink!

Charred cumin green beans with a mint and yoghurt sauce Serves 4

These green beans were inspired by some sugar-snap peas I had at a restaurant called Gjelina, in Los Angeles (see, I told you I'd been on a real holiday!). They're a brilliant side dish for a barbecue, or you can mix them with some fresh spinach or other salad greens for a delicious salad – great with some torn chicken on top for my carnivorous friends.

200g green beans, fresh or frozen • 1 tablespoon oil, sunflower or groundnut, plus a little extra to serve • 1 teaspoon cumin seeds or ground cumin or garam masala • 2 fat cloves of garlic, finely chopped • a few sprigs of mint • 150g natural plain yoghurt • a fistful of parsley or coriander, to serve • zest of ½ lemon or 2 teaspoons bottled lemon juice, to serve • a pinch of chilli flakes, to serve

If using frozen green beans, rinse them thoroughly in warm water to defrost, then blast with cold water. (My mum always told me that hot water wasn't clean enough to drink, so I'm a bit fastidious about rinsing veg in it.) Top and tail fresh beans.

Heat the oil in a frying pan, or better still, a griddle pan if you have one. Toss in the green beans and cumin or garam masala and cook over a high heat until the beans are softened and charred in places.

Meanwhile, peel and finely chop the garlic. Finely chop the mint leaves. Stir the garlic and mint into the yoghurt. Roughly chop the coriander or parsley, discarding any tough stalks. Serve the beans atop your chosen herb, with the yoghurt drizzled over, a little extra oil, a grating of lemon zest or a dash of juice, and a scattering of chilli flakes.

Pasta with creamed herring roe and green beans

This recipe was inspired by a similar one in Jocasta Innes's *The Pauper's Cookbook*, kindly sent to me by a reader of my *Guardian* column – and very gratefully received; I had been looking for a copy for quite some time, but to no avail. Herring roe is inexpensive to buy in tins and, with its strong, distinctive flavour, a little goes a long way.

Serves 2

1 onion

a small knob of butter, or 2 tablespoons oil, sunflower or groundnut

a fistful of fresh parsley, plus extra to serve

125g tin of herring roe in brine

100ml cream or natural yoghurt

salt and pepper

150g spaghetti

100g green beans, fresh or frozen

a fistful of spinach or other salad leaves (optional)

½ lemon

Peel and chop the onion. Heat the butter or oil in a frying pan, add the onion and cook over a low heat for 8–10 minutes until softened and translucent.

Meanwhile, roughly chop the parsley, discarding any thick stalks. Drain the herring roe and tip it into a blender, with the cream or yoghurt and parsley. Season well and pulse until smooth. Add it to the pan with the onion and let it warm through.

Bring a pan of salted water to the boil, and feed in the spaghetti. Cook according to the packet instructions, usually around 8–10 minutes. Add the green beans for the last 2 minutes.

Drain and rinse the spaghetti and beans, then add them to the pan with the creamed roe. Toss everything together, then warm through.

Serve as is, or atop a pile of green leaves – spinach works well here, wilting slightly under the hot pasta. Garnish with parsley and a generous squidge of lemon juice.

Three-ingredient pasta sauce

This simple recipe is easy to make your own – the sweetness of the softened garlic means there's no need to add sugar to the tomatoes. I save my empty jam jars in a drawer in the kitchen for things like this – see page 262 for advice on sterilizing jars.

Makes 1 large jar

6 fat cloves of garlic, or 10 smaller ones

50g butter

1 x 400g tin of chopped tomatoes

Peel and finely chop the garlic, then toss into a saucepan with the butter. Pop it over a very low heat, stirring constantly to melt the butter and soften the garlic. Don't rush this step: it's a labour of love – burned sticky bits of garlic will ruin your sauce.

When the garlic is soft, pour in the chopped tomatoes and stir through. Bring it to the boil, then boil vigorously for 1 minute, still stirring so the tomatoes don't stick to the bottom of the pan. Then reduce the heat to a very low simmer and leave for 20 minutes, stirring occasionally.

This sauce improves with a long cooking time, so although it will be ready to use after 20 minutes, consider cooking it for longer to thicken and develop. Or leave it to cool, spoon it into a jar and put it into the fridge.

Feel free to customize this sauce as you wish – a diced red pepper tossed in with the garlic at the beginning will add sweetness and extra flavour, or an onion to pad it out, or play with some herbs – rosemary or thyme or mixed dried herbs for a rich Italian flavour, parsley or basil for a fresh summery sauce. I like it best just as it is, with a generous pinch of salt and a good grinding of black pepper.

Double the recipe and pop half into the freezer, either in a jar or in an ice-cube tray for convenient portions.

This is one of those recipes where a slow cooker comes into its own. Put the finely chopped garlic with the butter and tomatoes into it, and cook on a high heat for 1 hour, then reduce to low for 3 hours. When I'm making sauces in my slow cooker, I put all of the ingredients into a roasting bag and tie the top: first, they don't spread thinly across the bottom and make a sticky burned mess; second, I don't have to clean the slow cooker; and third, I can pop two or three different bags in at once and make the most of having it on!

Delia's gazpacho   **Serves 3–4**

Most of the time I cook based on what I have in the cupboard or fridge, throwing together weird and wonderful concoctions, experimenting and exploring to come up with new ideas. And sometimes I delve into my shelf of cookery books and consult one of the experts. I'm no expert, really: I just do what I love and love what I do. Delia Smith, however, is a great British institution, and her gazpacho recipe (from *The Complete Illustrated Cookery Course*) is ten times better than anything I've managed to come up with so far. So, Delia, thank you. I've made some tweaks to suit my cooking style, but don't we all?

½ cucumber • ½ onion (Delia uses spring onions) • 2 fat cloves of garlic • 1 red, orange or yellow pepper (Delia uses ½ a pepper) • 2 x 400g tins of chopped tomatoes (that's a tweak, can you tell?) • a few basil leaves or sprigs of parsley • 4 tablespoons oil, sunflower or groundnut (Delia uses olive) • 1–2 teaspoons caster sugar, to taste • 1 tablespoon wine vinegar • salt and pepper

Dice the cucumber. (You can peel it, if you like, but it isn't necessary.) Peel and finely slice the onion. Peel and crush the garlic. Deseed and chop the pepper. Reserve about a quarter of the chopped vegetables and cover them with cling film. Put the rest, with the tomatoes, in a blender. Chop enough basil or parsley to fill 1 teaspoon. Add the basil or parsley, oil, sugar, vinegar and seasoning.

Blend everything at top speed until the soup is absolutely smooth. Taste to check the seasoning, adjust if necessary with more salt and pepper, and pour into a large bowl. Stir in a little cold water to thin it slightly – 150–275 ml/5–10 fl. oz. Cover with foil and chill thoroughly.

When you're ready to serve, ladle the soup into the bowls. Either scatter over the reserved vegetables or pass them round for everyone to help themselves.

Butch romesco

Romesco is a nut and red pepper-based sauce, made traditionally with almonds, but I use peanuts or cashews in mine, as that's what I tend to have in the house. I add extra garlic and a dash of vinegar for a punch, and keep it big, bold, butch and chunky. For a twist on the traditional, chargrill a bunch of spring onions until soft, sweet and blackened round the edges, and dunk them in the sauce with your fingers. In Catalonia they do this with calçots, but they're not too common round these parts . . . You can cook this dish in the oven or on the hob, whichever you prefer.

Serves 4

100g unsalted peanuts (or thoroughly washed salted ones) or cashews or almonds

4 fat cloves of garlic

1 large red pepper

4 tomatoes

4 tablespoons oil, sunflower or groundnut

2 slices of bread (optional)

2 teaspoons white wine vinegar or cider vinegar

Preheat the oven, if roasting, to 180°C/350°F/gas 4.

Roughly chop the nuts. Peel and chop the garlic. Deseed and dice the pepper. Chop the tomatoes.

If you're roasting it, toss them all into a roasting tin, pour 1 tablespoon of the oil into the tin and mix so that all the vegetables are coated. Then roast for 30 minutes, until the peppers and tomatoes are charred round the edges.

If you're cooking on the hob, put 1 tablespoon of the oil in the frying pan over a high heat, add the nuts, garlic, peppers and tomatoes, and cook for 10 minutes or until the peppers and tomatoes are charred round the edges.

Allow the veg to cool. Tear the bread, if using, and toss it with the veg, the rest of the oil and the vinegar.

To be roughly chopped or slung into a blender with a generous pinch of salt. Stir through with the remaining oil to loosen and chill before serving/storing.

TIP: Also delicious spread on sourdough toast with charred spring onions on top. For a more traditional romesco sauce, make with almonds instead of peanuts, but I like the boldness of the peanut flavour with the sweet roasted peppers.

Sweet and sour chicken

This recipe is from my 'Ready Meal Revolution' series published in the *Guardian*, where I dissected and reconstructed popular takeaways and ready meals to see if I could make them cheaper, healthier and tastier. Okay, so it's not quite as easy as dialling the local Chinese and getting it delivered to your door, but it's pretty simple.

Serves 4

300g boneless chicken thighs

1 tablespoon oil, sunflower or groundnut

1 onion

2 fat cloves of garlic

1 fresh red chilli, or a pinch of dried chilli flakes

2 tablespoons white wine vinegar

200g carrots, fresh or tinned and drained

a thumb of fresh ginger

1 x 230g tin of pineapple

70g tomato purée

salt and pepper

First, dice the chicken into manageable chunks. Heat the oil in a medium saucepan and toss in the chicken to brown and seal. Stir to stop the pieces sticking to the bottom of the pan.

When the chicken is golden, lift it out of the pan on to a plate and set it aside. Peel and dice the onion, peel and finely chop the garlic, and slice the chilli, if you're using a fresh one. Toss them into the pan (add the dried chilli flakes, if using), with the vinegar, and sauté over a medium heat until softened. Wash the fresh carrots, if using, then slice them. Cut tinned ones into chunks. Peel and grate the ginger – you need ½ teaspoon.

Tip the pineapple, including the juice, and the carrots, into the pan, then stir in the tomato purée and grated ginger.

Bring to a vigorous boil, then reduce to a simmer for 20 minutes to cook the chicken through and thicken the sauce. Taste, and season.

TIP: For a vegetarian alternative, replace the chicken with diced peppers or broccoli – or any vegetables you fancy.

Pork and prune burgers

These little beauties started off as meatballs when we had friends over for dinner and only had some sausagemeat and sad little prunes with which to make a miracle meal. I liked them so much that I made them again as burgers, and now they're a staple in our household. Mess around with the recipe – change the herbs, add some chilli, spice them up – you won't go far wrong!

Makes 6

6 prunes

1 onion

a fistful of coriander or mint or parsley

400g pork mince

a pinch of nutmeg

2 rounded tablespoons flour

2 tablespoons oil, sunflower or groundnut

Slice the prunes, removing any stones. Peel and chop the onion. Remove any thick, tough stalks from the coriander, mint or parsley and chop it. Put them with the pork mince into a mixing bowl. Season, then add the nutmeg and flour. Mix everything together thoroughly with your hands or a wooden spoon.

Cover the mixture and chill for at least 30 minutes – or, if you're in a rush, add an egg and an extra rounded tablespoon of flour to bind.

Shape the mince mixture into 6 burgers. Heat the oil in a frying pan, then fry the burgers for 7–8 minutes on each side over a medium heat until cooked through.

TIP: If you don't have any prunes, you can substitute sultanas. Put them into a little water and ping them in the microwave for 30 seconds to fatten them up so they're lovely and juicy.

Piccalilli   **Makes 2 good-sized jars**

Piccalilli reminds me of my father who always had a jar in the fridge at home when I was a child. I would surreptitiously steal the tangy, mustardy little onions from it – sorry, Dad! I've not used baby onions in mine, because they're hard to find and even harder to peel, so just grab a regular onion and dice it roughly for a piccalilli that's easier to spread. And less attractive to small children who might like to pick out the baby onions. You can mess around with the quantities, depending on what you have. As long as it's a good mix of oniony things, long things and cauli, you can't go far wrong.

1 onion • 1 small fresh cauliflower or 200g frozen florets, defrosted • 1 cucumber or 1 courgette, or 1 of each • 1 rounded tablespoon flour • 1 teaspoon turmeric • 1 teaspoon cumin • ½ teaspoon salt • a good grinding of black pepper • 500ml wine vinegar • a scant teaspoon of mustard, English or Dijon, but wholegrain will do • a fistful of fresh coriander

Peel and roughly dice the onion, and cut the cauliflower into small chunks. Remove the seeds from the cucumber and dice it. Dice the courgette, if using. Toss the veg into a saucepan with the flour, spices, salt and pepper, and give it a good stir. Pour in the vinegar and add the mustard. Bring to the boil, then turn down the heat and simmer for 15–20 minutes until the cauliflower and other veg are tender.

Allow to cool. Chop the coriander, discarding any tough stalks, and stir it in. Spoon into warm sterilized jars and screw on the lids.

It's ready to eat immediately, but improves with a little age – hence the quantities in the recipe: you can have some for now and some for later, or even some to give away.

TIP: See page 262 for advice on sterilizing jars.

Tomato and onion salsa

Makes 1 jar

I love a good tomato salsa, smeared on top of burgers or thinned with a little oil to dunk chips or potato wedges into, or spooned into a jacket potato with a dollop of soured cream as a side dish for a barbecue. It's incredibly simple to make – here's my no-frills version.

1 onion • 1 red pepper • 1 tablespoon oil, sunflower or groundnut • 6 whole prunes • 1 x 400g tin of chopped tomatoes • 1 tablespoon white wine vinegar • a pinch each of salt and pepper • a fistful of flat-leaf parsley or coriander • ½ lemon

Peel and finely chop the onion. Chop the red pepper, discarding the seeds and white membrane. Heat the oil in a frying pan. Add the onion and the red pepper and cook until they've softened, for 8–10 minutes. Chop the prunes and throw away the stones. Add the tomatoes and prunes to the pan. Tip in the vinegar and simmer for 15 minutes. Season. Chop the parsley or coriander, if using.

Squeeze over the lemon juice and sprinkle with your chosen herb.

Peach and lime crumble

Apart from the butter, which is usually stored in the fridge or butter dish, this is essentially a store-cupboard dessert, my favourite kind! Use fresh peaches, cooked with a little sugar and water, if you prefer, but I like the simplicity of the canned variety, cut through with a little lime to give a lift to the sweetness.

Serves 4

200g flour
100g sugar
100g oats
150g butter
1 fresh lime
1 x 400g tin of peaches in syrup
1 tablespoon honey
cream, ice-cream, custard or yoghurt (optional) to serve

Preheat the oven to 180°C/350°F/gas 4.

In a bowl, combine the dry ingredients. Melt the butter in a pan or a microwave and stir into the dry ingredients to form a breadcrumb texture. Add 2 tablespoons of water and mix it in carefully – don't overdo it as you'll end up with porridge rather than a crumble topping. Leave to one side.

Grate the lime zest and squeeze out the juice. Pour the peach slices into an ovenproof dish with half of the syrup from the can. Don't cut them up or they'll disintegrate into mush. Drizzle over the honey, then the lime juice. Top with the crumble and the lime zest.

Bake in the centre of the oven for 30 minutes until golden.

If you like, you can serve it with cream, ice-cream, custard, or yoghurt sweetened with a little sugar, or eat it warm and plain.

TIP: I use a generous amount of oats to make a rough and chunky crumble. If you prefer a more crumbly crumble, replace half of the oats with flour.

Charred peaches with cream cheese and coffee

I can't remember where I got the inspiration for this recipe – it's a scrawled note in the back of a very old Moleskine recipe book, one of my first but not the first, which was lost somewhere in twelve house moves. I sobbed when I realized it was gone. However, seven remain, filled with scribblings and ideas, recipes and tweaks, in varying degrees of neatness – this was just a few words in a large looped circle at the back of one. I made it for the first time in the summer, when I was kicking ideas around for this book. It took one attempt: the sticky sweet syrup on the peaches charred and caramelized, the cream cheese melted, and the kick of the coffee scattered on top cut through the sweetness for a pleasantly burned aftertaste. Win, win, win.

Serves 4

a small knob of butter

1 x 400g tin of peach halves in syrup

100g cream cheese

100g natural yoghurt

1 teaspoon freshly ground coffee, or instant will do

Heat a medium frying pan and drop in the butter. Drain the peaches, reserving the syrup.

Place the peaches in the hot butter and sizzle for a few minutes, turning regularly to stop them sticking, until the edges crisp and blacken.

Beat a little of the reserved peach syrup into the cream cheese and yoghurt to loosen. Place the peaches on 4 saucers, top each with the cheese mixture and a smattering of coffee. Serve immediately.

Courgette chocolate cake

Courgettes in cake came into vogue a few years ago, but I only really bothered with them when I had a glut of the green blighters last autumn. Desperate to get rid of them, I made them into wholesome soups, pestos, pasta sauces and smuggled a few into this big chocolate cake.

Serves 6–8

2 courgettes

50g dark chocolate or cocoa powder

zest of 1 lime

250g self-raising flour

75g sugar

a pinch of salt

75ml oil, sunflower or groundnut, plus extra for greasing

3 eggs

Preheat the oven to 180°C/350°F/gas 4.

Wash the courgettes and grate them into the centre of a clean tea-towel. Wring out as much moisture as you can over the sink – they hold a lot and you don't want to end up with mush instead of cake.

Grease a loaf tin. Grate the chocolate, if using. Grate the zest from the lime.

Put the flour, cocoa powder or grated chocolate, lime zest, sugar and a pinch of salt into a large mixing bowl. Mix thoroughly.

Make a well in the centre of the dry ingredients and pour in the oil. Add the courgettes and crack in the eggs. Stir well to combine, then pour the mixture into the loaf tin. Bake for 40 minutes or until a knife inserted in the middle comes out clean.

TIP: If you fancy a variation, try adding a selection of chopped nuts or dust with icing sugar and grated lime zest.

Courgette ribbons

Courgette ribbons look fancy and gorgeous, but are extraordinarily simple to make. I've used them as a pasta substitute and as a salad, and often when I've had a few sad courgettes kicking about and wanted to do something cold and refreshing with them. I like to mix them with spaghetti, but you can leave them as a salad, if you like. Courgette ribbons two ways – hooray!

Serves 2

150g spaghetti (optional)

2 fat cloves of garlic

1 fresh red chilli or a pinch of dried chilli flakes

zest and juice of 1 lemon

a fistful of mint

1 tablespoon oil

salt and pepper

2 courgettes

If you're using the pasta, put a pan of water on to boil, then pop in the spaghetti and cook according to the packet instructions, usually around 8–10 minutes. The next few stages take mere minutes, depending on your dexterity with a vegetable peeler, so it should all come together around the same time.

Finely chop the garlic and slice the fresh chilli, if using. Grate the zest from the lemon and squeeze out the juice. Pick the mint leaves and chop them. Mix together the garlic, chilli, fresh or dried flakes, lemon zest and juice, oil and half of the mint. Season with salt and pepper and stand to one side.

Cut the very top and bottom from the courgettes – I give the bits to the guinea pig, a handy little kitchen waste unit.

Using a vegetable peeler, slice each courgette into long ribbons from top to bottom. Sweep lightly for very thin ribbons, or apply a little pressure from your wrist for slightly more substantial ones – up to you. Keep going until you have no courgette left and a pile of pretty ribbons.

To make the salad, toss the ribbons with the remaining mint, pour over the dressing, and serve.

If you're using the pasta, pop the ribbons into the spaghetti pan before you drain it, then drain. Tip the pasta and ribbons back into the saucepan, add the dressing and toss thoroughly with the rest of the mint. Serve.

Cheat-roasted garlic hummus

I love hummus – as a snack, to dip vegetables into or smeared on a chunk of bread for a quick, lazy snack. A pot of it doesn't last very long in my house. The cheat-roasting works for anything you want a little bit of soft, sweet garlic in, without turning the oven on to roast a few poxy cloves . . .

Makes 1 bowlful

1 bulb of garlic

4 tablespoons oil, sunflower or groundnut

1 x 400g tin of chickpeas

1 lemon or 2 tablespoons bottled lemon juice

a pinch of salt

Divide the garlic bulb into cloves, and rub each with a tiny smudge of oil. Pop into a microwave-proof dish and ping on full power for 20 seconds. Open the microwave door, close and repeat – and there you have soft, sweet garlic that tastes like it's been roasted in the oven for 40 minutes rather than pinged in the microwave for 40 seconds.

Next, drain, rinse and mash your chickpeas in a bowl with a fork or masher. Some people like to pick the skins out as they loosen for a smoother hummus, but I like mine rough and chunky, so it's up to you. Squeeze the soft garlic in from each clove, add the lemon juice, oil and salt, and mash some more to combine.

Eat straight away with chunks of bread, or chill until needed. It will keep in the fridge, covered, for up to 3 days, but may need a little oil to loosen it again if it dries out.

Garlic soup

A whole bulb of garlic to yourself in a soup might sound intimidating, but slowly roasted and blended with cream and butter it's subtle and sweet, not overpowering. You can cheat-roast the garlic in the microwave instead of in the oven: see the Garlic Hummus recipe opposite.

Serves 2

2 bulbs of garlic

1 large onion

1 tablespoon oil, sunflower or groundnut

salt and pepper

a few sprigs of fresh thyme or 1 teaspoon mixed dried herbs

1 tablespoon butter

500ml chicken stock

200ml cream

25g hard, strong cheese

1 lemon, to serve

Preheat the oven to 180°C/350°F/gas 4.

Break the garlic bulbs into cloves. Peel and quarter the onion. Toss the garlic and onion into a roasting dish with the oil, a few pinches of salt and a grinding of pepper. Cover the roasting dish with foil, and cook on the middle shelf for 30 minutes, or until the garlic cloves are soft and tender.

Transfer the garlic to a plate or bowl and leave until cool enough to handle. Pick enough leaves from the thyme, if using, to fill 1 teaspoon. Gently melt the butter in a saucepan, and squeeze out the garlic from each clove into the pan. Toss in the onion and stir together. Pour over the chicken stock and add the thyme or mixed herbs, bring to the boil, and remove from the heat.

Pour into a blender with the cream and blitz until smooth. Grate the hard, strong cheese. Pour the soup into bowls. Scatter over the cheese and add a squeeze of lemon. Serve.

SEP | OCT

02

---

aubergine | cauliflower | blackberries
| apples | potatoes | squashes

In September 2013, I was offered a weekly recipe column with the *Guardian*, writing budget recipes for the Thursday edition of *G2* magazine. Suddenly I wasn't just a 'food blogger' any more, but a weekly recipe columnist for a national newspaper – and one I happened to quite like too! It featured recipes like the aubergine curry on page 56, and the frozen berry yoghurts on page 73.

Aubergine, pepper and Greek cheese tortilla

I like my tortillas cold and thick, the more veg-packed the better. You can stuff them with leftover veg or herbs and chopped leaves. Here I've gone for aubergine and pepper, with a crumble of salty cheese and a lot of black pepper – but go wild with whatever you fancy, or whatever you need to use up quickly!

Serves 2

1 aubergine

1 onion

1 pepper, red, green, yellow or orange

3 tablespoons oil, sunflower or groundnut

a fistful of parsley

4 eggs

50g Greek-style cheese (goat's, feta, etc.)

salt and pepper

Dice the aubergine, discarding the ends. Peel and chop the onion. Deseed and dice the pepper. Pop them all into a medium pan with 2 tablespoons of the oil and cook over a medium heat for 8–10 minutes until soft. Tip into a bowl.

Chop the parsley, discarding any tough stalks, and stir it into the veg. Beat in the eggs. Crumble the cheese into the bowl and mix through, taking care not to break it up too much. Season well.

Pour the rest of the oil into the pan and let it warm – it shouldn't sizzle or splutter – then pour in the eggy-veg mixture. Give it a quick stir, pause for 20 seconds, and give it another quick stir. Cook for 2–3 minutes on each side until the egg is done.

Either eat hot and fresh, or leave to cool completely and pop into the fridge for a handy snack.

Smoky aubergine, tomato and red lentil pasta sauce

Like so many of my recipes, this one came about from a sad-looking vegetable in the fridge, with the realization that it was probably past its best and needed to be eaten Straight Away, or else be consigned to the guinea pig – and even he turns up his nose at the state of some of the things in my fridge. I don't know how it happens – I buy vegetables, I use vegetables, but some are left to roll around in the bottom of the drawer and need a little help by the time they're at the brown-squashy-patch stage. So, in short, this is a great recipe for aubergines slightly past their best, but for an even better pasta-sauce experience, use fresh ones. This sauce is a hit with the small people in my household: they once demanded it for dinner three nights running. Little did they know how many vegetables were getting smuggled into their tiny bodies. Success!

Serves 3–4

1 large aubergine

4 fat cloves of garlic, or 6 smaller ones

1 onion

50g butter

500g tomatoes

a generous pinch of salt

zest and juice of 1 lemon

150g red lentils

a fistful of fresh coriander or parsley

Preheat the oven to 220°C/425°F/gas 7. Pop the aubergine into the oven and leave for 30 minutes until the flesh is soft and the skin is charred.

Meanwhile, peel and finely slice the garlic, then peel and chop the onion, if using. Toss them into a medium saucepan with the butter. Cook over a low heat for 8–10 minutes, until they have softened, stirring occasionally to stop them sticking to the bottom of the pan. Chop the tomatoes, discarding the cores.

When the onion is soft and translucent, add the chopped tomatoes, salt, lemon zest and juice, and stir well. Bring to the boil, boil vigorously for 1 minute, still stirring, reduce the heat to a simmer and continue to cook. Give the lentils a quick spritz under the tap, put them into the sauce, and stir.

When the aubergine is ready, remove it from the oven and allow it to cool. I pop mine into a bowl to catch the juices, then tip them into the sauce for extra flavour. When it is cool enough to handle, split the aubergine, scrape out the flesh and discard the skin. Dice the flesh and throw it into the sauce. Stir well, mashing the aubergine with a fork to combine. Simmer until the lentils have softened. To serve, chop the herbs, discarding any tough stalks, and scatter them over.

TIP: For the kids, I blitz it in the blender to make a smooth sauce before serving – making the vegetables unidentifiable and the sauce easier for little mouths. I serve theirs with a generous fistful of Cheddar on top, and goat's cheese or feta for any grown-ups. If you don't want to eat it straight away, it will keep in the fridge for 1 week, or in the freezer for 3 months.

Aubergine and kidney bean burgers

I love a good veggie burger, and probably have a veggie-burger recipe up my sleeve for every seasonal vegetable of the year – but these are an absolute favourite. Canned kidney beans make up the inexpensive bulk, adding protein and fibre, while the aubergines are tender, moist and smoky. Play with the spices: I've used chilli and cumin, but turmeric, curry powder, paprika, garlic, coriander or whatever you have will work well. Run as wild as your store cupboard will let you!

Makes 4–6

1 large aubergine or 2 little ones

1 onion

1 fresh chilli or a generous pinch of dried chilli flakes

4 tablespoons oil

1 teaspoon ground cumin

1 x 400g tin of kidney beans

a fistful of mint

juice of 1 lime or 1 lemon

3–4 rounded tablespoons flour

salt and pepper

Dice the aubergine, discarding the ends. Peel and finely slice the onion. Slice the fresh chilli, if using. Heat 2 tablespoons of the oil in a medium frying pan. Toss in the aubergine, onion, chilli, fresh or dried flakes, and the cumin and cook until the vegetables have softened for 8–10 minutes.

Drain and rinse the kidney beans.

Strip the mint leaves from the stalks and chop the leaves. Tip the kidney beans into a bowl and scrape in the now-soft aubergine and onions. Add the mint, then squeeze over the lime or lemon juice and mash well with a fork or masher. Stir in 2 tablespoons of the flour to thicken and season generously.

Pop the mixture into the fridge for 30 minutes to firm – this will stop it falling apart when you come to fry it. (If you haven't time for this, crack an egg into the mixture and stir it in with another heaped tablespoon of flour, and perhaps another. It should stick to the underside of your wooden spoon in a clump, but not be too dry or crumbly.)

With damp hands, shape the mix into 8 small patties, 4 mammoth ones, or whatever size you wish. Heat the remaining oil in a large frying pan and fry for 5–6 minutes on each side, over a medium heat, to cook through (slightly longer for bigger ones, shorter for smaller ones), turning as necessary, until browned and crispy on the outside and warm in the middle.

TIPS: You can serve these in so many different ways – with rice or chips, or a green salad, or in a bun, with a dollop of something sweet like mango chutney or ketchup.

Cometh the barbecue season, cometh the burger. You can shape these and open freeze them – pop them on to a baking tray, uncovered, for a few hours in the freezer, then transfer to a freezer bag. Get them out to defrost an hour or two before you need them, then fling them on to the barbie. Yum!

Melitzanosalata

I gave this recipe as a tip in *A Girl Called Jack*, at the bottom of the Baba Ghanoush recipe, and was inundated with requests from readers for a more comprehensive recipe. Here it is!

Serves 2

1 large aubergine

4 fat cloves of garlic

juice of 1 lemon
or 2 tablespoons
bottled lemon juice

2–3 tablespoons oil,
sunflower or groundnut

a pinch each of salt
and pepper

Preheat the oven to 200°C/400°F/gas 6.

First, pierce the aubergine all over with a small sharp knife, and pop on to a baking tray.

Bake in the centre of the oven, until the skin is charred and the aubergine is very soft, for approximately 35–40 minutes, but it may take longer depending on the size. Wrap the garlic cloves in foil and roast alongside the aubergine for the last 30 minutes.

When cooked, leave the aubergine and garlic to stand for around 10 minutes until cool enough to handle. Some of the aubergine juices will drain out, so you might want to pop it in a colander in the sink to avoid a sticky mess.

When it is cool enough to handle, quarter the aubergine lengthways and scrape the soft flesh into a small bowl. Mash any lumps with a fork. Squeeze the garlic cloves into the bowl, stir in the lemon juice and oil, and season with salt and pepper.

Best served at room temperature, but it can be covered and chilled in the fridge.

TIPS: If using a fresh lemon for the juice, finely grate the rind over the top of the dish to give it a pop of colour and to lift the flavour – entirely optional but if I'm using fresh lemons, I want to use the whole thing! Also good with some chopped coriander stirred through.

To make it go further, use it as a base for cooked red lentils, to make a smoky pasta sauce (see page 52).

Jonaki's baba gosht

One of my favourite Indian takeaway shops in my former hometown, Southend-on-Sea, made this fabulous lamb and aubergine curry that they called Baba Gosht. When doing my research for this book, I came across lots of recipes for Baba something or other, and lots of recipes for various Goshts, but never anything by the same name. So, this is my approximation of what I used to get from the Jonaki Tandoori, and, just for you, I ate about ten portions of it along the way, just to make sure I got it right . . .

Serves 2 generously

2 large onions

4 fat cloves of garlic

1 fresh red chilli

300g lamb neck or fillet

1 large aubergine

a thumb of fresh ginger or ½ teaspoon ground ginger

2 tablespoons oil, sunflower or groundnut

2 bay leaves

½ teaspoon cinnamon

½ teaspoon turmeric

1 teaspoon cumin seeds or ground cumin

a pinch of salt

1 x 400g tin of chopped tomatoes

300ml water

a fistful of coriander, to serve

Peel and finely slice the onions. Peel and chop the garlic. Slice the fresh chilli. Dice the lamb, removing any fatty or sinewy bits. Dice the aubergine, discarding the ends. Peel and grate the fresh ginger, if using – you need 1 teaspoon.

Heat the oil in a large pan over a medium heat. Toss in the bay leaves and let them sizzle to release their flavour. Reduce the heat to low, and add the cinnamon, turmeric, ginger, cumin and salt. Fry for 1 minute, then add the onions, garlic and chilli. Stir to combine, and cook over a low heat for around 8–10 minutes to soften the onions. Keep stirring to prevent the onions sticking to the bottom of the pan – burned onions will permeate and ruin your curry: you want soft, sweet ones that melt to form the sauce.

Add the lamb and the aubergine. Continue to cook over a low heat, stirring regularly so that the meat is sealed on all sides, then pour over the tomatoes and 200ml of water. Crank the heat up to bring it to the boil, then boil vigorously for 1 minute, and reduce the heat. Cover and simmer for 30 minutes, or until the lamb is tender. Check periodically and add a splash of water if it starts to dry out.

Chop the coriander, discarding any tough stalks. Scatter generously to serve. Some Indian bread or fluffy basmati rice would go well with it.

Spiced cauliflower, butter bean and almond soup   Serves 4

This recipe is based on a scribbled note I found scrunched up and stuffed into my purse after a conversation over lunch with my friend Janet, who is excellent with food. It said, 'Janet soup. Cauli, b. bean, almond, pap/spice'. Two years on, here's my interpretation of 'Janet soup' – probably bearing no resemblance to the original, but still absolutely delicious.

1 large fresh cauliflower or 400g frozen florets, defrosted • 1 onion • 2 fat cloves of garlic or 3 smaller ones • 2 tablespoons oil, sunflower or groundnut • 1 fresh chilli or a pinch of dried chilli flakes, plus extra to garnish • 2 teaspoons ground cumin, plus extra to garnish • scant ½ teaspoon turmeric, plus extra to garnish • 1 x 400g tin of butterbeans or other white beans – baked beans, rinsed, are a great cheap substitute • 25g ground almonds • 750ml chicken stock or water • salt and pepper

First, cut the cauliflower, fresh or frozen, into small florets, and finely slice the onion and garlic. Put them into a medium pan, with the oil, chilli, cumin and turmeric, then fry over a medium heat until the onion has softened and the cauli is a nutty brown, for 8–10 minutes.

Drain and rinse the beans, tip into the pan, and stir in the ground almonds. Pour over the chicken stock, and bring to the boil. Season, then reduce to a simmer and cook for 10–12 minutes until the cauliflower is tender and the beans have softened.

Blitz in the blender until smooth, then pour the soup back into the pan with a splash of water, if necessary, to reach the desired consistency. Reheat thoroughly, then pour into bowls and garnish with a shake of cumin and turmeric, the chilli and a scattering of fresh coriander, if using.

Cauliflower, ginger and turmeric salad

This salad is inspired by one I ate for lunch in Brighton while visiting for a political party conference. Unusually for me, I didn't jot down in my notebook the name of the shop where I bought it. It was a big gorgeous deli somewhere near the sea, with large windows, and this bright goodness caught my eye. I bought a small dish of it, went and sat on the sea wall and tucked in, making notes as I went along. You can pad it out with little pasta shells, or leave it light as a salad, a side or a snack. Apologies to the big-gorgeous-deli people: I'll be back to find out who and where you are next time I'm there!

Serves 2

a thumb of fresh ginger

50ml oil, sunflower or groundnut, plus a little extra to coat the cauliflower

½ teaspoon turmeric

1 small fresh cauliflower or 200g frozen florets, defrosted

100g green beans, fresh or frozen and defrosted

a generous fistful of spinach or rocket leaves

a squeeze of lemon juice

a fistful of fresh coriander or parsley

To make the dressing, peel and finely grate the ginger – you need 1 teaspoon. Pour the oil into a small saucepan, and add the turmeric with the ginger. Warm over a low heat for 2–3 minutes to flavour the oil – it will turn a delicious autumnal yellow. Remove from the heat and allow to cool – you can make the dressing up to a day in advance.

Remove the outside leaves and the tough stalk from the fresh cauliflower, then break it into florets. Top and tail the green beans, if using fresh. Coat the cauliflower with a little oil, and toss in a very hot pan with the beans for 8–10 minutes or until the cauli is golden and the beans soft and slightly charred round the edges.

Remove from the heat and allow to cool.

To serve, drench the vegetables with the dressing and toss them with the spinach or rocket. Add a squeeze of lemon juice and the coriander or parsley. Serve immediately.

TIP: For a more substantial dish, mix the salad with cooked and cooled rice, pearl barley or lentils. To make it a bit posher, add a handful of flaked almonds, toasted with a little chilli, to serve.

Roasted cauliflower, fennel and garlic soup

Serves 2

This wholesome, earthy soup is packed with flavour from the sweet roasted onions and unmistakable taste of fennel. I used fennel seeds in mine, but if you have a fennel bulb rolling around in the bottom of the fridge, slice it and add it with the cauliflower, potato and onion.

1 potato • 1 onion • 1 large cauliflower or 400g frozen florets, defrosted • 4 fat cloves of garlic or 6 smaller ones • a scant teaspoon of fennel seeds • 2 tablespoons oil, sunflower or groundnut • 500ml chicken or vegetable stock

Preheat the oven to 200°C/400°F/gas 6.

Peel and dice the potato. Peel and quarter the onion. Discard any outer leaves and the tough stalk from the fresh cauliflower and divide it into florets. Put the vegetables into a large roasting dish.

Bash the garlic cloves, in their skin, with a rolling pin or wooden spoon, and add to the roasting dish.

Combine the fennel seeds with the oil, pour over the vegetables and give everything a good stir to distribute the oil evenly. Roast for 20 minutes.

Remove from the oven. Squeeze the garlic out of its papery skin and transfer everything to a blender, ensuring you scrape in the oil and fennel seeds.

Pour over enough stock to cover and blend until smooth. Reheat the soup and serve.

TIP: The leftover soup makes a delicious pasta bake. Simply thin it with a little water, milk or stock, pour over some pasta, with a fistful of strong grated cheese, and bake in the centre of the oven at 180°C/350°F/gas 4 for 20 minutes, or until the pasta is cooked and the cheese is golden and crispy.

Cauliflower mac 'n' cheese with bacon

This is part mac 'n' cheese, part cauliflower cheese, and deliciously golden and moreish with some crispy bacon thrown in for good measure. Baking it at the end to melt the cheese isn't essential, but, oh, it's so good.

Serves 4

300g short pasta, like macaroni

2 tablespoons oil

200g cauliflower, fresh or frozen, grated or broken into small florets

200g streaky bacon, chopped

2 eggs

200ml milk

black pepper

100g hard, strong cheese

Bring a medium saucepan of water to the boil. Add the pasta and reduce to a simmer.

Meanwhile, gently heat the oil in a large saucepan, then add the grated cauliflower and bacon.

In a separate bowl, beat together the eggs, milk and pepper. Add a few tablespoons of the pasta cooking water and beat in.

When the pasta is al dente, drain it and add to the pan with the cauliflower and bacon. Pour in the egg mixture and mix through.

Transfer to an ovenproof baking dish, top with the grated cheese and grill for a few minutes, until the cheese is golden and crispy.

Berry bircher breakfast pot

I made this imitation of a breakfast pot I saw in a high-street coffee shop, then worked out that it had cost a sixth of the commercial price. I included a pumpkin-seed and cranberry adornment in homage to the original, but it works well with any mixture of dried fruit and nuts you have at your disposal. You can defrost the mixed berries by giving them a quick spritz under the cold tap.

Serves 2 – they look small but they're incredibly filling!

50g porridge oats

200g natural yoghurt

50g frozen mixed berries

1 level teaspoon (approx. 20) pumpkin seeds

1 level tablespoon (approx. 20) dried cranberries and sultanas, or other dried fruits or nuts of your choice

Combine the oats, yoghurt and defrosted berries in a bowl. Add a splash of water if it's a little thick. Spoon into two ramekin dishes or portable pots (I find those pots that value soft cheese comes in, with the snap-on lid, are a great size). Top with the pumpkin seeds and dried fruit.

Eat immediately, or chill in the fridge and eat within 2 days.

TIP: For a better berry bircher, make them the night before and chill in the fridge – the oats will soften and swell, making them easier for kids to eat too.

Autumn puddings

I used to live in an area that was rife with blackberry bushes, so I would go out foraging with gloves, plastic containers and small helpers when I could. If you don't have a succulent bushy haven to hand, poke your face into the freezer department of your local supermarket for a smorgasbord of juicy goodness all year round.

Makes 4

400g berries, fresh or frozen

75g sugar, plus extra to serve

2 tablespoons water

8 slices of white bread

a fistful of chopped fresh mint (optional)

a shake of lemon juice (optional)

cream or yoghurt, to serve

If you're using frozen berries, pop them into a large bowl or plastic container and sprinkle over the sugar, then leave them to defrost at room temperature for a few hours or in the fridge overnight. If you're using fresh berries, give them a quick spritz under the tap, pop them into a large bowl or plastic container, cover with sugar, add the water, and leave for 1–2 hours to let the berry juices run out – you'll need them to soak the bread. To speed up the process, mash them a bit with a fork. Chop the mint, if using.

Line 4 x 175ml pudding tins with cling film – not essential but it helps when turning out the puddings.

Remove the bread crusts. Cut 2 slices of bread in half and set aside: these will be the tops of the puddings. Now cut 4 squares slightly larger than the bottom of each tin for the base, and rectangles for the sides from the remaining bread – you may need a bit of trial and error to see what fits. A few millimetres of overlap is fine, as you can mash it down with your fingers, but gaps and holes are not, so err on the side of big ones.

Place a sieve over a bowl and drain the fruit to collect the juice. Dip each piece of bread into the juice briefly to colour one side – don't make it soggy. Line the bottom of the dish with the coloured side facing downwards, and build up the sides, coloured sides outwards, pressing the edges together to seal.

If using, stir the mint and lemon juice through the berries. Spoon the berries into the middle of the pudding, compacting the fruit tightly. Spoon any remaining juice into each tin, then cover the top with the remaining soaked bread, and seal closely with cling film. Place tins on a baking tray, with plates or a tray on top. Weight it down with tins of beans, tomatoes or whatever. Chill for at least 2 hours or overnight to set.

Turn out the puddings on to plates, with extra sugar and some mint and lemon slices to garnish, if you like that sort of thing. Serve with cream or yoghurt.

Burned brown-sugar meringues with blackberry yoghurt

Makes 6 medium-sized meringues or 4 great big ones

Demerara and caster sugar behave very differently in cooking: sometimes you can get away with substituting one for the other, and sometimes you can't. When I first made meringues (Mother's Day, 2014), I couldn't help but wonder, in my own mischievous way, if I could make them with different kinds of sugar. Getting right the ratio of caster to demerara took three or four attempts, but they were experiments I was quite happy to make!

4 eggs • 150g caster sugar • 150g demerara sugar • 1 teaspoon cornflour, or ordinary flour will do • 1 teaspoon white wine vinegar, cider vinegar or rice vinegar

For the yoghurt: 200g blackberries (or any berries) • 200ml natural yoghurt • zest of 1 lemon • few mint leaves

Preheat the oven to 130°C/250°F/gas ½. Take a baking sheet or two, and line with greaseproof paper.

Separate the eggs, and put the yolks to one side. (You can freeze them individually in an ice-cube tray and add them to an omelette or scrambled eggs, or pop them into the fridge and make a quick custard out of them at some point over the next 2 days.)

Whisk the whites until they form stiff peaks – this is one of those occasions where an electric mixer of some description comes in handy, but if you don't have one, persevere and change arms every few minutes!

When the whites have stiffened, add the caster sugar, a tablespoon or two at a time, and beat it in. Then beat in the demerara sugar, a tablespoon at a time. When all the sugar is in, the mixture will be thick and glossy. Add the cornflour, then the vinegar, and beat again.

Dollop the meringue mixture upwards on to your trays (to form a pretty curl on top), a very heaped tablespoon at a time, shaking gently to loosen the mixture. If I'm feeling impatient, I point the spoon downwards and use two fingers to scrape the mixture off – it makes a messy, modern-art-style meringue.

Bake in the centre of the oven for 1 hour AND DO NOT OPEN THE DOOR. Leave these babies well alone! Then turn off the oven, still without opening it, and keep the door shut. Leave the meringues in there for another hour or so, until the oven has cooled completely, then remove. They are ready to eat, or you can store them in an airtight bag or container for up to 3 days.

To serve, chop the blackberries and stir them into the yoghurt until it marbles with the purple juice. Spoon some on to each meringue, then grate over the lemon zest and decorate with a few mint leaves and some extra berries.

Of course, the meringues are absolutely delicious eaten on their own as a snack, without the trimmings . . .

Blackberry and white chocolate frozen yoghurt lollies

I first made these berry desserts with foraged blackberries, but any berries will do. Bags of mixed frozen ones are often far cheaper than their fresh counterparts, and are perfect for this simple dessert. The smallest girl in my household loves these lollies, and as they are essentially berries, cheese and yoghurt (with a little bit of contraband chocolate), I'm more than happy to make them for her.

Makes 4 ramekins or lolly moulds

100g white chocolate
100g mixed frozen berries
150g soft cream cheese
300g low-fat natural yoghurt

Break up the chocolate and melt it gently in a mixing bowl over a pan containing 4cm of boiling water. Make sure the water doesn't touch the bowl: too much heat will make the chocolate bitter.

Remove the bowl from the heat, using a tea-towel or oven glove.

Add the berries, cream cheese and yoghurt and stir well to combine until smooth – the cheese will soften into the chocolate and yoghurt.

Spoon into ramekin dishes or lolly moulds, and freeze for at least 2 hours.

Lollies can be served as they are. Ramekins should be removed from the freezer 20 minutes before eating to thaw, or pinged in the microwave for 1 minute to soften a little.

Bramley apple jelly

I was given a crate of Bramleys last year by a group of farmers who had a bumper crop that they were unable to sell. I smuggled them into breads, into my apple and cinnamon cake, and still had more than I knew what to do with. So, I made apple jelly, and spent the next few months dolloping it on to crackers with cheese, smearing it over pork, using it as a base for stews and sausage casseroles and even as a sweet, sticky sauce for stir-fried vegetables, with a dash of vinegar or soy sauce. This recipe also works for crab apples, or any other apples.

Makes around 6 jars, depending on the size of your jars . . .

1kg apples

zest and juice of 1 lemon, or 4 tablespoons bottled lemon juice

550ml water

1kg sugar

First, pop a saucer or two into the freezer. You'll need these for testing if the jelly has set later on.

Wash the apples and chop them roughly. There is no need to peel them, but you might want to core them, especially if you plan to use the 'slush'. (My friend Andree and I made a huge batch of crab apple jelly one year, then recycled the apple slush, after the juice had dripped through the muslin, into a compôte for a doubly satisfying result.) Toss them into the bottom of a large pan – stock-pot-sized is best as the mixture bubbles right up the sides.

Grate the lemon zest into the pan, being careful to avoid the pith, or it will make your jelly bitter. Squeeze the lemon juice into a small bowl and set it aside.

Add the water and bring to a gentle boil. Simmer very gently until the fruit is soft and mushy, which usually takes around 30 minutes, depending on how ripe your apples were and how small or large you chopped them.

Line a sieve or colander with a piece of sterilized muslin, a clean pillow-case or thin tea-towel. (To sterilize, simply iron with a hot-hot iron, and don't put it down somewhere dirty immediately afterwards!) Lay it over the top of another saucepan or a bucket, and pour the cooked fruit into it to drip through. This will take 1–3 hours – jelly-making is not for people with complicated schedules! If you've started making it in the evening, you can leave it overnight. If you're an impatient soul, you can shove it through with a masher, but it's hot, hard work, and your jelly will be cloudy for it.

When all the juice has dripped into the pan, measure it in a measuring jug to find out how much sugar you need. Add 1g of sugar for every 1ml of liquid.

Pour the juice back into the pan, and heat gently with the sugar. Pour in the lemon juice. Bring slowly to the boil, and boil for around 20 minutes before testing.

Meanwhile, unscrew the lids from your jars and lay them on their sides on a baking tray. Place them in the oven and turn it on to 150°C/300°F/gas 2. When the oven is hot, turn it off, but leave the jars inside until you need them. To sterilize plastic lids, wash them in the hottest water you can handle, remove, and wrap in a clean tea-towel until needed.

To test whether or not the jelly is set, remove one of the saucers from the freezer, and place a teaspoon of boiled liquid on it. Leave it for 1 minute, then push it gently with your finger. If it's set, the top will wrinkle slightly. If it isn't, continue to boil it. Test again after 10 more minutes – this process can take up to 1 hour.

When the jelly is at setting point, ladle it into the jars. Handle them carefully, with a doubled tea-towel on your hand, as they will be hot! Put on the lids immediately and leave to cool.

Label, and store in a cool, dry place.

Bramley apple soda bread

This is another recipe made from my generously donated crate of Bramley apples. Delicious with any kind of cheese – I've had it with Brie, blue and mature Cheddar and can vouch for all three – and cakey enough to fool the kids . . .

Serves 4

200ml milk

2 teaspoons lemon juice

200g flour, plain or rye or wholemeal, plus a little extra for dusting

1 rounded teaspoon bicarbonate of soda

1 large Bramley apple, approx. 250g

a little butter, for greasing

Preheat the oven to 180°C/350°F/gas 4.

Measure out the milk, add the lemon juice and leave to stand.

Put the flour into a mixing bowl, add the bicarbonate of soda, and quickly stir it through.

Cut the apple into quarters and remove the core. Finely dice or grate the quarters – I leave the skin on mine for extra goodness, and it adds a nice crunch to the bread. Peel it, if you like, but you'll be missing out on a treat! Mix the finely diced or grated apple into the flour.

Pour in the soured lemony milk, and stir well. It should have the consistency of batter, not dough. Lightly grease and flour the inside of a loaf tin, then pour in the mixture.

Bake in the centre of the oven for 40 minutes, until golden brown and a skewer comes out clean. Allow to cool for 5 minutes before turning out of the tin.

TIPS: This recipe works just as well with non-dairy milk. Almond or hazelnut would be a delicious nutty alternative, and soya milk is fine too. I used 2 heaped teaspoons of milk powder in 200ml cold water. I can never tell the difference in cooking, but I can definitely tell the difference in my wallet!

Customize the apple soda bread with whatever flour you like. Rye flour gives a heavy, flavourful loaf. Wholemeal flour supplies an earthy texture, complemented by the sweetness of the apple. Gluten-free flours work just as well, but you may need to add a little extra liquid. Once you've chosen your flour, why stop with apples? You could try substituting berries, bananas, sultanas, fresh herbs . . . Be brave!

Apple crumble granola

This decadent-tasting breakfast is simple to make, and you can use any combination of fruit and spices that you have to hand. Frozen berries with chunks of white chocolate, banana and cinnamon, even grated orange rind and dark chocolate for a luxury twist – the possibilities are endless.

Makes 6 servings

300g oats

1 apple

30g butter, plus a little extra for greasing

1 tablespoon honey

1 teaspoon ground cinnamon

Preheat the oven to 180°C/350°F/gas 4.

Tip the oats into a mixing bowl, and grate the apple over the top – I leave the skin on for extra goodness. Stir it into the oats quickly to prevent the apple from browning as it comes into contact with the air.

Pop the butter into a microwave-proof dish and ping on a high heat for 20 seconds to melt. Add the honey and cinnamon to the melted butter and stir, then pour into the oat and apple mixture, and stir again thoroughly.

Lightly grease a baking tray or roasting dish, and tip in the oat mixture. Even it out with a spoon, but don't press down: you want it to clump together in chunks, not make a flapjack. Pop it into the centre of the oven for 30 minutes, shaking it gently halfway through.

Allow to cool completely, then put it into an airtight container. It will keep for a few weeks if stored in a cool dry place.

Bombay potatoes

**Serves 2 generously,
or 4 as a side dish**

1 onion

2 fat cloves of garlic

a thumb of fresh ginger

1 small fresh red chilli
or a pinch of dried
chilli flakes

1 tablespoon oil

2 teaspoons garam masala

140g tomato purée

the scant tip of a
teaspoon of mustard

500g potatoes – tinned are
quick and cheap

a fistful of fresh coriander

This recipe was another part of my foray into dissecting and replicating readily available convenience food. I tried to make my versions cheaper, healthier and tastier – and this simple dish is one of my favourites. If you are using tinned potatoes, it will be super-quick and easy to make.

First, make the sauce by peeling and dicing the onion. Peel and finely chop the garlic. Peel the ginger and grate enough to fill ½ teaspoon. Slice the chilli, if using a fresh one. Put them all into a saucepan with the oil. Sprinkle over the chilli flakes, if using, and the garam masala, then cook over a low heat for 10 minutes, or until softened. You really don't want to burn your onions or garlic in this one – yeuch.

When the onions are soft, stir in the tomato purée and the mustard, with a splash of water to loosen.

Wash and dice the potatoes, and add to the sauce. Bring to a vigorous boil, then reduce to a gentle simmer for 5 minutes (tinned) or 25 minutes (fresh) to cook through.

Remove from the heat. Chop the coriander, discarding any thick stalks, then stir into the pan. Serve.

TIP: This freezes really well. Spoon leftovers into an airtight container or freezer bag, allow to cool completely and store in the freezer for up to 3 months. You can defrost in the microwave, or in the oven at 180°C/350°F/gas 4 for 30 minutes.

Sleepy potatoes

If I could pick just one recipe that said 'comfort food', this would be it. I'd normally serve this as a side dish to roast chicken, but I'm also happy with the leftovers, cold in a bowl on its own, curled up in front of the fire of an evening, or in a corner of the sofa. I call them sleepy potatoes in homage to the coma-inducing carb hit and satisfying creamy texture. Bliss.

Serves 4

2 large leeks

2 large potatoes or
2 x 500g tins of potatoes

a little butter, oil or
margarine, for greasing

100g hard, strong cheese

4 fat cloves of garlic

200ml cream

200ml milk

salt and pepper

a good grating of nutmeg

Preheat the oven to 180°C/350°F/gas 4.

Strip the hard outer layer from each leek and discard – or chop and freeze to add to a stock pot somewhere down the line. Then thinly slice the leeks, white and green parts.

Thinly slice the potatoes (without peeling them, if you're using fresh – the skin is the best bit!).

Lightly grease a ceramic baking dish, and place a layer of spud slices in the bottom. Scatter leeks on top, then more spuds and leeks in layers until they're all in, finishing with a layer of spuds. Grate the cheese and top with a generous handful.

Peel and chop the garlic. Stir together the garlic, cream, milk, remaining cheese, and seasoning, then pour into the dish. Grate a little nutmeg over the top.

Bake at 1 hour in the middle of the oven. Serve hot!

TIP: Leftovers are delicious tossed through pasta for a double-carb hit, with chopped cooked bacon.

Smoky roe

Herring roe has a strong flavour all of its own – if you're not sure you'll like it, try the recipe with some plain white fish first. I use tinned potatoes in this dish, as they're much cheaper than fresh. You can, of course, use whatever spuds you like – just parboil them first. The delicious smoky combination of flavours is a real winner in my house for a simple chuck-it-together supper.

Serves 2

2 sprigs of fresh parsley

3 tablespoons oil

1 tablespoon lemon juice

a generous shake of smoked paprika

500g cooked potatoes

1 onion

120g herring roe

100g green beans, fresh or frozen and defrosted

Preheat the oven to 180°C/350°F/gas 4.

Make the marinade. Chop the parsley finely. Put it into a bowl with the oil, lemon juice and smoked paprika, mix well, then set to one side.

Next, dice the potatoes and scatter them in the bottom of a roasting dish. Peel and chop the onion and layer it over the top.

Place the pieces of herring roe between the potatoes and onions and pour over the spiced lemony oil, then toss together to coat.

Roast for 25 minutes, taking the dish out halfway through to shake it, turn the contents, and add the green beans.

TIPS: Leftovers will keep in the fridge for 2 days in an airtight container, if allowed to cool completely, and can be eaten cold, as a delicious potato salad, or reheated.

Soft herring roe is gorgeous on toast too. Spread it with a little lemon and black pepper.

Aunty Helen's potato sandwiches

As a child, I spent many a summer afternoon bouncing about in the back of my parents' Land Rover on a six-hour drive down the coast to Plymouth, to visit Aunty Helen. She had a house with a secret annexe and garden, and two great big geese, Charlie and Geraldine, which used to chase us shrieking and honking around the garden. The highlight of the trip was always the potato sandwiches that were hot and ready for us on our arrival, just in time for us small ones to go to bed.

Serves 1

1 large potato
salt and pepper
1–2 tablespoons oil
2 slices thick white farmhouse bread
softened butter, to spread

Thinly slice the potato, with its skin, and season with salt and pepper. Heat the oil in a large frying pan, and fry the potatoes for 6–8 minutes on each side over a medium–high heat, in batches if necessary, until crisp and cooked through.

Wedge between the well-buttered bread slices.

TIP: Add some brown sauce or pickle for added tang.

Squash and thyme risotto

You can use any orange root vegetable for this risotto – carrots, sweet potato, squash or even pumpkin. I like it with hard, strong cheese sometimes, but cream cheese and goat's cheese work well too. If you have any spare mushrooms lurking in the back of the fridge, throw them in for a complementary earthy flavour, and bacon would be another great addition.

Serves 4

1 butternut squash

a fistful of fresh rosemary or thyme, or 1 scant tablespoon dried mixed herbs

3 tablespoons oil, sunflower or groundnut

1 onion

4 fat cloves of garlic

350g rice

a knob of butter

1 litre chicken stock

100g hard, strong cheese

Preheat the oven to 200°C/400°F/gas 6.

Peel and dice the butternut squash, discarding the seeds. Pick the leaves from your chosen herb, chop and then throw them, or the dried mixed herbs, into a roasting dish with the butternut squash and 2 tablespoons of the oil. Roast for 45 minutes until tender and crisp round the edges. Give the dish a good shake every now and again so that it cooks evenly.

Meanwhile, peel and finely chop the onion and garlic. Heat the remaining oil in a medium frying pan, add the onion and garlic, and sweat over a low heat for 8–10 minutes to soften the onions and sweeten the garlic, stirring every now and again.

When the onions have softened, add the rice and butter. Stir until the butter has melted, and turn up the heat.

When the ends of the rice grains are translucent, pour over a little stock, around a quarter of it, turn down the heat and leave it to absorb. When the rice has drunk up all the liquid, add another quarter and stir. Repeat until all the stock is used up and the rice is tender and soupy.

Take the squash out of the oven and stir it into the rice, mashing any really tender pieces into the risotto with a fork or wooden spoon, but leaving some chunks.

Remove from the heat and allow to rest for a few minutes. To serve, grate the cheese and scatter over the top.

TIP: Serve with a fresh green salad.

Squash and cheese bread

This warming autumnal bread can be made with any orange root vegetable. If you don't fancy the rigmarole of grating a hard, unwieldy butternut squash, you can try it with sweet potato or carrot instead.

Makes 1 loaf

1 small butternut squash

50g hard, strong cheese, plus a little extra for scattering

4 tablespoons black olives, plus a few extra for scattering (optional)

a fistful of fresh rosemary or thyme or sage or 1 tablespoon dried mixed herbs

300g self-raising flour, plus a little extra for dusting

a pinch of salt

2 eggs

a splash of milk

Preheat the oven to 190°C/375°F/gas 5.

Lightly grease or line a baking tray – no loaf tin required for this one!

Peel the butternut squash, cut in half, discard the seeds and grate the flesh. Grate the cheese. Slice the olives, if using. Pick the leaves from the rosemary, thyme or sage and chop enough to fill 1 tablespoon. Tip the flour and salt into a large mixing bowl, and add the squash, cheese, olives and your chosen herb. Mix briefly to combine.

Make a well in the centre, and crack in the eggs. Splash in the milk and mix to form a large ball of dough. If it's too dry, add another splash of milk; if it's too sticky, add 1–2 heaped tablespoons of flour – use your judgement. It should be slightly tacky to touch, but not impossible to get off your fingers.

Shape the dough into a loaf and place it on the baking tray. Dust it with a little flour, scatter some grated cheese on top, make a cut down the middle with a sharp knife, and stud with olives if you're feeling fancy. Bake in the centre of the oven for 45 minutes, until it feels fairly light and sounds hollow when you tap the bottom.

NOV | DEC
03

kale | chestnuts | winter roots

In November 2013, Richard Littlejohn from the *Daily Mail* wrote a full-page article saying that I couldn't ever have been properly poor because I made a kale pesto. I wrote a letter back to him, pointing out sixteen basic facts he had got wrong about me in one article, and the letter went viral, such is the way of the internet. I gained an extra 8,000 followers on Twitter, and a determination to grow my own kale just to annoy anyone who thinks that it's a luxury of some sort. The Kale Pesto recipe that caused such a storm is on page 108, and you can read the letter on my blog; it's still one of my most-read articles to date. I scratched it out on my mobile phone in my pants at ten past seven in the morning, proving you don't need to be dressed or caffeinated to battle trolls – especially professional ones. Aside from kale and controversy, November and December seem like fairly barren months when it comes to fresh fruits and vegetables, but keep your eyes peeled for the 'stew packs' of mixed root vegetables that make an appearance in the supermarkets – I use them to make all sorts of yummy soups and winter vegetable salads.

Also in this chapter: Charity Curry Night

CHARITY CURRY NIGHT

In November, I held the first of my Charity Curry Nights, with my friends Juliet and Jim, borrowing their big gorgeous kitchen for the occasion!

The format is simple: cook lots of curry as cheaply and deliciously as possible, charge people a certain amount per head for an all-you-can-eat curry buffet, and donate the money to charity. We tend to raise between two and three hundred pounds a time, splitting the money between good causes, like our local food bank and homeless shelter.

We all have a good night. I get to cook a lot and watch lots of people tuck appreciatively into their dinner which is always very satisfying – and we raise some cash for good causes into the bargain.

If you want to hold your own charity curry night, you'll find some recipes in this book to get you started, and more on my blog.

Fish korma

Serves 4

2 fat cloves of garlic or 4 smaller ones

2 onions

1 small fresh red chilli or a pinch of dried chilli flakes

400g white fish fillets

1 tablespoon oil

2 teaspoons ground cumin

2 teaspoons turmeric

200g creamed coconut

100g sultanas

500ml low-fat natural yoghurt

a fistful of fresh coriander

Peel and finely slice the garlic. Peel and chop the onions, and finely slice the fresh chilli, if using. Cut the fish into bite-sized chunks. Heat the oil in a large saucepan or frying pan, then add the onions, garlic, fresh or dried chilli, the cumin and turmeric. Sweat over a very low heat for 8–10 minutes until the onions have softened.

Add the creamed coconut, sultanas and a mug of water, and turn up the heat. Stir to dissolve the coconut and absorb the spices into the mix. Add an extra half-mug of water if you feel it needs it – your mugs and my mugs might be different sizes!

When the coconut has melted, add the fish and cook for 5 minutes. Remove the pan from the heat. Stir in the yoghurt – don't reheat or the sauce will split.

Chop the coriander, discarding any thick stalks. Serve, with coriander scattered over the top.

TIPS: Adjust the spices according to taste. I like this dish mild, sweet and creamy, but it could take an extra teaspoon of cumin and another chilli for a kick.

To make it go further, add some diced new potatoes and/or a couple of fistfuls of frozen green beans.

Banana, tea and chickpea curry

1 onion • 2 fat cloves of garlic, or 4 smaller ones • 1 fresh red or green chilli or a generous pinch of dried chilli flakes • 1 tablespoon oil, sunflower or groundnut • 1 teaspoon ground cumin • ½ teaspoon ground cinnamon • 300ml strong tea • 1 x 400g tin of chickpeas • a fistful of coriander, mint or parsley • 2 bananas • 1 x 200g tin of mandarins (peaches or apricots would work too) • 200ml natural yoghurt, plus extra to serve

Peel and finely slice the onion. Peel and finely chop the garlic. Slice the fresh chilli, if using. Put the onion, chilli, fresh or dried flakes, and garlic into a pan and drizzle over the oil. Add the cumin and cinnamon, then cook gently over a medium heat to soften the onions, 8–10 minutes.

Meanwhile, boil the kettle and brew the cuppa! (Make one for yourself while you're there!) Drain and rinse the chickpeas thoroughly. Chop the coriander, mint or parsley, discarding any thick stalks. Peel and slice the bananas.

When the onions have softened, tip the chickpeas into the pan. Drain the mandarins, reserving the juice (add it to the curry if it starts to dry out, or you can put it into a salad dressing: see page 18), and throw them into the pan with the bananas. Pour in the tea (without the teabag) and add most of your chosen herb – saving a little to use as a garnish. Turn the heat up high and boil vigorously for 5 minutes. Reduce the heat and simmer for another 20 minutes, until the sauce has thickened slightly. To save energy, you can turn off the heat instead of simmering: cover the pan with foil or a lid and leave it. The retained heat will continue to cook it gently, amalgamating the flavours beautifully.

Just before serving, stir through the yoghurt, and scatter over the remaining coriander, mint or parsley. Serve with rice and/or pitta bread, with some more natural yoghurt on top.

Curried eggs

Serves 2

4 eggs

1 onion

1 fresh red chilli or a pinch of dried chilli flakes

1 tablespoon oil, sunflower or groundnut

2 teaspoons turmeric

2 teaspoons ground cumin

200g rice

100g spinach, frozen or fresh

1 x 400g tin of chopped tomatoes

100g natural or Greek yoghurt

First, fill a pan with water and carefully drop in the eggs. Bring to the boil, then reduce to a simmer for 10 minutes to hard-boil them.

Meanwhile, peel and chop or slice the onion, according to your preference. Slice the fresh chilli, if using. Heat the oil in a frying pan and add the spices. Cook for 1 minute, then add the onion and chilli, fresh or dried, and cook for 8–10 minutes over a medium heat until it has softened.

Remove the eggs from their pan when they are done, and plunge them into cold water to cool. Add the rice to the egg water – saves you boiling more – and cook according to the packet instructions, for around 12–15 minutes. Wash and pick over the fresh spinach, if using.

Pour the chopped tomatoes over the spicy onions, add the spinach and stir. Bring to the boil, then reduce the heat and leave to simmer while the rice cooks. (To save energy, you can turn off the heat and cover the pan with foil, a lid or a large plate – the curry sauce will carry on cooking but will need a quick blast of heat before serving.)

Peel and halve the eggs and add to the sauce with the yoghurt. Stir them in gently and heat through.

Serve with the rice.

TIP: Mango chutney is a great addition to this dish, if you have a jar kicking about the place.

Fish tagine

Serves 4

300g rice

1 onion

1 tablespoon oil, sunflower or groundnut

1 teaspoon ground cumin

1 teaspoon paprika

1 vegetable or chicken stock cube

a few sprigs of mint or coriander

4 white fish fillets

1 x 200g tin of mandarin segments

1 x 400g tin of chopped tomatoes

a fistful of sultanas

150g spinach

Bring a pan of water to the boil, then put in the rice and cook according to the packet instructions, for around 12–15 minutes. Peel and chop the onion. Heat the oil in a frying pan over a medium heat and add the onion. Sprinkle in the spices and crumble over the stock cube, then cook for 8–10 minutes until the onions have softened.

Chop the mint or coriander, discarding any tough stalks. Add the fish to the pan, then pour over the mandarins, their juice and the tomatoes. Toss in the sultanas, your chosen herb and the spinach, stir gently, and bring to the boil for 1 minute. Reduce to a vigorous simmer for 15 minutes, stirring occasionally to stop the sauce sticking to the pan.

Meanwhile, check the rice. When it's cooked, remove it from the heat and drain.

Break the fish into chunks and stir through the sauce. Serve over the rice.

TIPS: Leftover mint can be chopped finely and frozen in an ice-cube tray with a splash of water or oil for handy portions, or hung upside down to dry out and stored in a jar.

This tagine works well with chickpeas and root vegetables, instead of fish, as a vegetarian alternative, or with chicken thighs and/or drumsticks.

Potato dhansak

Serves 4

100g red lentils
1 large onion
4 fat cloves of garlic
a thumb of fresh ginger
3 tablespoons oil,
sunflower or groundnut
1 small red chilli or
1 scant teaspoon of
dried chilli flakes
2 teaspoons ground cumin
1 teaspoon turmeric
a scant ¼ teaspoon
cinnamon
1 large potato
2 large carrots
400ml vegetable stock
1 x 400g tin of chopped
tomatoes
50g sultanas
a fistful of coriander,
chopped
zest and juice of ½ lemon

Pop the lentils into a sieve and rinse under cold running water.

Peel and finely slice the onion. Peel and chop the garlic. Peel and grate or finely chop the ginger. Heat the oil in a medium frying pan. Put in the onion, garlic and ginger and cook over a low heat for 8–10 minutes until the onion has softened. Slice the fresh chilli, if using. Add the fresh or dried chilli, cumin, turmeric and cinnamon to the pan and stir.

Peeled and roughly dice the potato and carrots, then drop them into the pan. Cook for a further 5 minutes, turning the heat up to medium, stirring to prevent the onions burning.

Pour over the stock and tomatoes, then add the lentils and sultanas. Stir, and bring to the boil. Boil vigorously for 1 minute, then reduce to a simmer for around 20 minutes, and cover with a lid, plate or foil. Stir from time to time to prevent it sticking to the pan. Chop the coriander, discarding any thick stalks.

When the lentils are cooked and the sauce has thickened, grate over the lemon zest, squeeze over the juice, stir in the coriander and serve.

Little mouths may prefer this with a few generous tablespoons of plain yoghurt stirred through to calm the heat!

Channa masala

**Serves 2 as a main dish,
4 as a side**

1 x 400g tin of chickpeas

1 onion

1 fat garlic clove

1 fresh red chilli or
1 teaspoon dried
chilli flakes

4 tablespoons oil,
sunflower or groundnut

1 teaspoon cumin

a fistful of
fresh coriander

1 x 400g tin of
chopped tomatoes

Drain the chickpeas, and rinse thoroughly.

Peel and finely chop the onion, garlic and fresh chilli, if using. Heat the oil in a saucepan, then toss in the onion, garlic, fresh or dried chilli and the cumin. Sweat over a very low heat for 10–12 minutes until the onions are sweet, spicy and translucent.

Finely chop the coriander, discarding any thick stalks, and set it aside.

Pour the chopped tomatoes over the onions, stir through and cook for a further 10 minutes until the sauce is thick and glossy.

Stir in the chickpeas and coriander, then heat through, and serve.

TIP: This is also delicious made with yellow split peas, but soak them first for at least 8 hours, or overnight. Cook them for about 30 minutes, until they are soft, and add to the sauce as you would the chickpeas.

Spiced split pea and yoghurt soup

Serves 4

100g yellow split peas

1 onion

2 fat cloves of garlic
or 4 smaller ones

2 carrots

1 tablespoon oil

1 teaspoon ground cumin
and 1 teaspoon turmeric
or 2 teaspoons
garam masala

100g yoghurt

salt and pepper

a fistful of parsley
or coriander

First, pop the dried yellow split peas into a bowl and cover with water, then with cling film or a plate, and leave to soak for at least 8 hours, or overnight.

Peel and finely chop the onion and garlic, and peel and slice the carrots. Heat the oil in a medium-sized saucepan, then toss in the onion, garlic and spices, and cook over a medium heat for 8–10 minutes until the onion has softened. Add the carrots and stir.

Drain and thoroughly rinse the split peas, and tip into the pan. Cover with water and stir well. Bring to the boil, then reduce the heat and simmer for 20 minutes, or until the split peas and carrots are soft.

Pour the mixture into a blender, tip in the yoghurt, and pulse until almost smooth. I like to leave mine a bit rough and chunky for a great texture, but it's up to you. Taste, and season.

Serve hot, garnished with torn parsley or coriander, and with bread to dunk.

TIPS: Replace the yoghurt with soy yoghurt, or almond or rice milk, for a real vegan treat.

Freeze leftovers in small portions to use as a spicy, chunky pasta sauce, or as the base for a curry with leftover chicken. Defrost the soup in a pan with a little water, stir in the chicken and any green veg you have to hand – I'm thinking green beans, broccoli or peas, fresh or frozen. It works just as well without the chicken – a colourful, healthy, sensationally quick dinner.

Kale pesto

I knocked together this kale pesto after I found a bag of dark green leafy goodness for 75p in the supermarket, blitzed it in the blender with some other bits and blogged about it, and was inundated with kale chips and in-jokes from friends for months afterwards. If you fancy a side order of controversy with your lunch, fling this lot into a blender and feel suitably mollified that you might be doing something cheap and healthy . . .

Makes 14 portions

200g kale

1 fresh chilli

80g hard, strong cheese

150ml oil, sunflower or groundnut, plus extra for sealing

150ml water

30ml lemon juice

Cut any tough stalks out of the kale. Slice the chilli. Grate the cheese. Stuff as much kale as you can fit into a blender (you can add more later). Throw in the rest of the ingredients, then blend until the kale has turned into a vivid green pulp. Turn the blender off. Add any remaining kale, and blend again.

Spoon the pesto into a clean jar, pour a little extra oil over the top to seal, and put on the lid.

TIPS: The kale pesto will keep in the fridge for up to 1 week. Alternatively, freeze it in ice-cube trays – no need for any oil on top.

You can serve it on spaghetti, with a pinch of extra chilli, or spread some on toast, top it with cheese and grill it.

Bacon kale bean thing

This simple dinner is a great way to pep up tired greens from the bottom of the veg drawer. Use whatever white beans you like – I often use baked beans and blast them under the tap to get rid of the tomato sauce: they're a third of the price of a tin of haricot or cannellini beans.

Serves 4

1 onion, finely sliced

2 fat cloves of garlic or 4 smaller ones

1 tablespoon oil

200g streaky bacon

1 x 400g tin of white beans

300ml chicken stock

2 tablespoons tomato purée

juice of 1 lemon or 2 tablespoons bottled lemon juice

100g green leaves: kale, spring greens or spinach

40g hard, strong cheese, to serve

Peel and finely slice the onion and garlic. Heat the oil in a frying pan, then add the onion and garlic. Cook over a low heat for 8–10 minutes until they have softened. Slice the bacon, then add it to the onions with the beans and stir through. Pour over the stock, stir in the tomato purée and squeeze in the lemon juice. Throw in the greens, stir them into the mixture, and let them wilt. Meanwhile, grate the cheese.

Serve with a fistful of cheese and some chunky bread.

TIPS: For a more substantial meal, add some pasta to the mixture while it's cooking with a little extra stock.

This is a dish that improves with a day in the fridge, allowing the flavours to develop. Heat through with a splash of extra water to loosen. It's a great place to drop that hard piece of cheese rind that usually ends up in the bin – toss it in with the onion at the start.

Chestnut risotto

I used to be quite intimidated by chestnuts. Having had no training in food, other than a decade or so of following my eyes and stomach, I know what I know based on impulsive decisions made in supermarkets and the contents of a fair few stuffed notebooks. If I don't know what something is or what to do with it, I bung it into a risotto while I work it out. There's not much that won't be complemented by creamy, soupy rice, and this is no exception. These days, I can do a lot more with a tin (yes, a tin) of chestnuts than a humble risotto, but this is so delicious that I had to include it. If you don't like chestnuts or can't get hold of them, use a few big handfuls of mushrooms instead for an equally good dinner.

Serves 2

1 onion

2 fat cloves of garlic

a fistful of thyme, or 1 scant tablespoon dried mixed herbs

2 tablespoons oil, sunflower or groundnut

100g bacon – smoked streaky is my favourite but any will do

200g rice

a knob of butter

100g chestnuts, tinned or vacuum-packed

800ml chicken stock

salt and pepper

50g hard, strong cheese

Peel and finely chop the onion and garlic. Pick the thyme leaves, discarding the stalks, and chop, if using. Heat the oil in a medium frying pan, then add the onion and garlic with the thyme, or the dried mixed herbs. Sweat over a low heat for 8–10 minutes to soften the onions and sweeten the garlic, stirring every now and again. Chop the bacon.

When the onions have softened, add the rice and butter. Stir to melt the butter, and turn up the heat. When the ends of the rice grains are translucent, add the bacon and chestnuts, and stir again.

Pour over a little stock, around a quarter of it, and leave to absorb. When the rice has drunk up all the liquid, add another quarter, and stir. Repeat until all the stock is used up and the rice is tender and soupy. Taste, and season.

Remove from the heat and allow to rest for a few minutes. Grate the cheese, scatter over the top and serve.

TIP: Don't have any thyme? How about topping with finely chopped sage for an earthy wintery flavour to complement the creamy chestnuts.

Chestnut and bacon soup

I don't make this soup at Christmas – I make it in the weeks following, when all the supermarkets reduce their tins of chestnuts, jars of cranberry sauce and goose fat to pennies in an effort to clear the shelves for Valentine's Day and the like.

Serves 2 generously

1 onion

2 fat cloves of garlic

25g butter or 2 tablespoons oil, plus a little extra for frying

a few sprigs of thyme or 1 teaspoon mixed dried herbs

200g chestnuts, tinned or vacuum-packed

500ml chicken stock

200ml cream or natural yoghurt

100g streaky bacon

salt and pepper

Peel and chop the onion and garlic. Heat the butter or oil in a saucepan, add the onion and garlic, and cook over a low heat for 8–10 minutes to soften, stirring occasionally.

Pick enough thyme leaves, if using, to fill 1 teaspoon. Add the chestnuts and thyme or dried herbs to the pan, cook gently for a few more minutes, then pour in the stock and bring to the boil. Reduce the heat to a simmer and cook for 10 minutes to soften the chestnuts.

Remove from the heat and tip into a blender. Pour in the cream or yoghurt and blitz until smooth. Leave to one side.

Dice the bacon. Give the saucepan a quick rinse, then add a smudge more oil, let it heat and add the bacon. Fry it over a high heat for 2 minutes or more, until it's as soft or crispy as you like. Remove from the pan and set aside a tablespoon to use as a garnish.

Pour the soup from the blender back into the pan to warm through – don't let it boil or it will split. Add the bacon, stirring to mix it in. Taste, and season.

Divide the soup between the bowls and scatter over the reserved bacon with a twist of black pepper.

TIPS: Leftover chestnuts can be made into chestnut flour, and stored in an airtight jar. Chestnut flour adds a sweet, nutty flavour to biscuits, breads, scones and muffins. It doesn't contain gluten, so it won't rise on its own, so instead replace 10–20% of your normal flour with it in a recipe.

To make chestnut flour from vac-packed or tinned chestnuts, pop them in the oven in a roasting dish at 180°C/350°F/gas 4 for 20 minutes to roast them and dry them out a little. Remove from the oven and leave to cool. Chop into small pieces, then toss into a blender and pulse until finely ground. Allow to cool completely, and tip into an airtight jar to store.

Roasted carrot and Greek cheese soup

Towards the end of a week in November, I had a glut of carrots, some cheap 'Greek-style cheese' (an imitation feta from the value range at the supermarket), plus other bits and bobs, and this was the result. Any leftover soup can be poured on to pasta with extra cheese crumbled over the top for a speedy lunch.

Serves 2

1 onion

1 tablespoon oil, sunflower or groundnut

1 potato

200g carrots

500ml chicken or vegetable stock

a fistful of coriander

100ml natural yoghurt

50g Greek-style cheese

Peel and slice the onion. Heat the oil in a saucepan, toss in the onion and cook over a medium heat for 8–10 minutes to soften.

Dice the potato and carrots, add to the pan, and pour over the stock. Bring to the boil, reduce to a simmer, and cook for 20 minutes until the vegetables are soft. Separate the coriander stems from the leaves, discarding any thick stalks, and chop both.

Pour the vegetables and stock into a blender, tip in the yoghurt and coriander stems, and blitz until smooth.

Pour into bowls, then scatter on the coriander leaves and crumble over the cheese. Serve.

Carrot fritters with a cumin and coriander yoghurt sauce

I love a fritter, especially as a cheeky, sneaky way to make veggies fun for the kids. What better than something that small hands can pick up and dip into a sauce, then cram into little mouths? Frying veg with cheese isn't an every-night-of-the-week option, but it's certainly an enjoyable way to do your vegetables. I make a simple zingy lemon and yoghurt dip for the small ones, and stir cumin into mine as an afterthought.

Serves 4

6 carrots
1 onion
1 egg
2 rounded tablespoons flour
50g hard, strong cheese
salt and pepper
oil for frying

For the sauce:
a good fistful of fresh coriander
150ml natural yoghurt
1 teaspoon cumin seeds
zest and juice of ½ lemon

Grate the carrots. Peel and finely chop the onion, then put it with the carrots into a large bowl. Crack in the egg and mix well, then add the flour and stir to combine. Grate in the cheese, season, and mix again.

Heat a little oil in a frying pan, and add a tablespoon of the fritter mixture. Flatten with the back of a spoon – the thinner they are, the faster they will cook and the crisper they will be. Fry on each side until golden and crisp. Remove from the pan and keep warm. Repeat until all the fritter mixture has been used.

To make the sauce, pick over the coriander and discard any thick stalks, then roughly chop it and stir into the yoghurt with the cumin seeds. Grate in the lemon zest, add the juice and stir well to combine. Serve immediately or chill until needed.

TIPS: The sauce can be made a day ahead and chilled in the fridge.

To keep each batch warm as you cook the rest, put them on a plate in the oven, heated to 140°C/275°F/gas 1. But they probably won't get that far!

Sweet carrot and nutmeg rice pudding

I make my rice puddings with long-grain rice as I don't often have pudding rice in the house, but you can make it with either. This recipe came about from a pile of carrots that needed using up (even with a guinea pig in the house!) and ever more inventive ways to do so . . . If you're a carrot cake fan, you can add a handful of sultanas to swell, and some chopped walnuts to the top. The smallest girl in my house loves this recipe, and she has excellent taste.

Serves 4

2 large carrots
500ml evaporated milk
500ml whole milk
2 tablespoons sugar
120g long-grain rice
a few pinches of grated nutmeg
25g butter
2 tablespoons honey

Grate the carrots and toss them into a blender with the evaporated milk, whole milk and sugar, and blend until mixed.

Tip the rice into the bottom of an ovenproof dish, and pour the milk and carrot mixture over the top. Bake in the centre of the oven for 30 minutes. Remove and stir, then grate over the nutmeg, dot with the butter and drizzle the honey over the top. Replace in the oven to bake for a further 30 minutes.

CHRISTMAS

04

Before I start, I feel compelled to issue a warning: I've thrown the turkey out of the window for this book (not literally, as that would be wasteful) and replaced it with a much smaller chicken. Firstly, I haven't had much cause for a sodding great turkey in recent years, and chickens are cheaper and easier to fit in the oven, with less carcass kicking around for the days that follow. Apart from that, I've been fairly traditional, with Yorkshire puds, mulled wine and sneaky sprouts snuck in . . . Christmas doesn't have to mean going mad and spending lots of money, but simple puddings such as pears poached in red wine prove that you don't have to splash out for a good, festive dessert.

Smoked mackerel pâté

In an effort to make an almost-traditional Christmas dinner for an episode of *The One Show* in 2013, I rustled up this speedy pâté with a few simple ingredients. Mackerel is one of my favourite fish – but you can use any smoked fish, salmon or even crab sticks.

Serves 4–6 as a starter

220g smoked mackerel
100g butter
100g cream cheese
juice of ½ lemon
½ teaspoon ground black pepper, plus a little extra to garnish (optional)
a fistful of flat-leaf parsley (optional)
6 slices of wholemeal bread
lemon wedges to garnish (optional)

First remove the skin from the mackerel – it should peel off easily – and discard. Put the fish into a large mixing bowl, and break up into flakes with a fork or wooden spoon and some elbow grease. Pick out any bones you can see – but small pin-bones are usually fine to leave.

Melt the butter in a microwave for 30 seconds (or in a saucepan), and pour it over the flaked mackerel. Add the cream cheese, lemon juice and pepper, then beat well to combine.

Press into a lightly greased tin (I find an old butter tub a good size for making pâté!) and chill in the fridge for at least 1 hour.

Chop the parsley, if using. To serve, put the bread (some like it toasted but I prefer mine soft and fresh) on a board in the centre of the table for people to help themselves. Turn out the pâté on to a plate and slice it. Scatter over the parsley, if using, or you could garnish it with wedges of lemon and a little more pepper.

Perfect Yorkshire puds

The trick to making perfect Yorkshire puddings is to get the fat really hot before you spoon in the batter. Then, once they're in, resist the urge to open the oven door or you risk flaccid puds. Nobody loves a flaccid pud.

Makes 6 in muffin tins or 1 large tin

2 tablespoons oil, sunflower or groundnut

125g flour

a pinch of salt

½ teaspoon dried mixed herbs (optional)

2 eggs

150ml milk

Preheat the oven to 200°C/400°F/gas 6.

Drop a little oil into the bottom of each muffin tin, or the whole lot into a large tin, and stick them straight into the oven to heat.

Tip the flour into a mixing bowl or jug (I mix my batter in a jug to make pouring it into the muffin tins or single tin easier). Add the salt and herbs, if using, and stir briefly to distribute.

Make a well in the centre of the dry ingredients – admittedly a bit more difficult in a jug than in a bowl but not insurmountable. Break in the eggs, pour in half of the milk and beat to form a smooth batter. Gradually beat in the rest of the milk.

Check your muffin tins or the large tin: the fat should be smoking hot. Pour or spoon in the batter until each muffin tin is around a third full, or tip the whole lot into a large tin, then return to the oven. Close the door and do not open it for 15 minutes. Be very strict about this!

Open the oven door after 15 minutes and serve pretty darn quick.

Tree biscuits

The last few Christmases had been all over the place for my little family, and 2013 was the first year I felt able to establish my own small traditions, which will hopefully carry on over the next few years. The first thing that sprang to my mind was making tree biscuits – although at the time I didn't have a tree to hang them on!

Makes 24, in assorted sizes

100g unsalted butter, plus a little extra for greasing

300g flour, plus a little extra for dusting

2 eggs

100g caster sugar

1 teaspoon ground cinnamon

icing sugar (optional), to dust

First, preheat the oven to 180°C/350°F/gas 4.

Now the butter: because I make these with my son, I cube it and melt it in the microwave for 60 seconds to make it easier to stir in. Traditionally, you would rub it into the flour with your fingertips, but once I started melting my butter in the microwave, I've never looked back. So, whichever method you choose, combine the butter with the flour to form a breadcrumb consistency.

Beat the eggs. Tip the sugar and cinnamon into the flour mixture, then beat in the eggs to form a dough.

Flour your work surface and hands, tip out the dough, and work it briefly to shape. Wrap the dough in cling film and allow to chill in the fridge for 30 minutes or until firm enough to roll out.

Once firm, roll it out on a floured surface – I don't own a rolling pin, so I use a clean, empty bottle, floured – to around 0.5cm thick for optimum biscuit thickness. Honest.

Cut out, using a cookie-cutter or, if you're feeling radical, a blunt knife to make whatever shaped biscuits you like. Re-roll the dough trimmings until all of it is used up. (Not one to promote brands too much, but I picked up most of my novelty cookie-cutters from Poundland and Ikea.) If you want to hang the biscuits on the tree, make a small hole, using a skewer or the tip of a sharp knife – the hole will need to be larger than you think, as it smooshes back together in the oven a little!

Lightly grease a baking sheet, and place your cookies on top, leaving a few millimetres around each one: they'll spread out and you don't want them to stick together. Bake in the centre of the oven for 12 minutes, until just golden and crisp. Take them out, and allow to cool on the baking sheet.

I dredge mine very lightly with icing sugar while warm, for an extra sweet kick.

Thread string or ribbon through, and hang them on the tree . . . if you think they'll last that long!

Pears poached in red wine

This recipe is so easy that it's hardly a recipe at all. I use tinned pears, because they're cheaper and easy to tuck away at the back of a store cupboard, and serve them in a bowl with ice cream and a little grated dark chocolate.

Serves 4

1 x 400g tin of pear halves

1 large glass of red wine

100g sugar, white or brown

a scant ¼ teaspoon of cinnamon

dark chocolate, to serve

Drain two-thirds of the juice from the pears and pour the remainder into a saucepan with the pear halves. Pour over the red wine, then add the sugar and cinnamon. Cover and poach for 15 minutes.

Remove the pears and set to one side. Bring the cooking liquid to the boil, uncovered, and boil vigorously until reduced by half.

Pop the pears into serving dishes, pour over the sauce, and grate the dark chocolate over the top.

Easy mulled wine

Mulled-wine recipes are varied and multitudinous, with everyone having their own twist on the traditional hot spiced festive drink. Here's my take on it, the way I've been making it for years – although I don't always add the Stone's Original Green Ginger Wine. I add extra fruit to impart sweetness and flavour, and strain it out before serving for a bonus dessert. The red wine you use shouldn't be too heavy – try a cheap Beaujolais, Fleurie, Brouilly or even a Tempranillo, or whatever you like. I'm not the wine police.

Serves 4

1 large orange or 1 x 200g tin of mandarins

100g sugar

6 cloves or a pinch of ground cloves

1 cinnamon stick or a scant ¼ teaspoon ground cinnamon

1 nutmeg or 2 pinches of ground nutmeg

1 x 750ml bottle of red wine

150g sultanas (if opting for the extra boozy fruit option)

50ml green ginger wine (optional)

Peel the orange to remove the rind, or drain the mandarins, reserving the juice. Put the peel or mandarin juice into a heavy-based saucepan.

Divide the orange into segments. Add the sugar, cloves, cinnamon and nutmeg to the pan, with a splash of water, and warm over a low heat, stirring well to prevent the sugar from burning. When the sugar has dissolved, pour in a small glass of the red wine, matched with a small glass of water, add the orange segments or mandarins and sultanas, and stir through. Bring to the boil, and reduce to a simmer for at least 20 minutes to allow the flavours to infuse.

Five minutes before you want to serve your mulled wine, pour in the rest of the wine and the ginger wine, if using. Warm through, but don't let it boil. Strain it through a sieve to catch the fruit, cloves and cinnamon stick. Serve.

For the boozy dessert, pick out the cloves and cinnamon stick from the strained gubbins, and you should be left with some boozy sultanas and orange segments or mandarins. Use them as the base for a festive crumble, or as the filling for some simple pies, or simply eat warm with a little brandy butter, cream or ice-cream.

'Special cabbage' with sneaky sprouts

Brussels sprouts: you either love them or you hate them, but if your only experience of them is as an accompaniment to your Christmas dinner, you should definitely give these a go. Sliced and pan-fried with cabbage and butter: this is how I smuggle them into the toddlers . . .

Serves 4 as a side dish

200g Brussels sprouts, fresh or frozen and defrosted

30g butter or a splash of oil

1 onion

4 fat cloves of garlic, or 6 smaller ones

½ savoy cabbage

salt and pepper

a grating of nutmeg (optional)

50ml cream (optional)

Slice or quarter the sprouts, discarding any tough outer leaves. Heat the butter or oil in a frying pan, toss in the sprouts and cook over a low heat. Peel and finely slice the onion and garlic, then add to the pan and stir well. Cook for 10 minutes to soften the vegetables, stirring occasionally.

Slice the cabbage, discarding any tough outer leaves and stalk, and add to the pan. Season well, and stir in. Turn up the heat and cook for a further few minutes until the edges of the sprouts are slightly golden. If you've opted for nutmeg and cream, add them now, and continue to cook for 2 more minutes. Serve hot.

Finnish-style liver casserole

Last Christmas I was challenged by the *Guardian* to cook a non-traditional budget Christmas dinner and looked around the world for inspiration. I fell in love with Finnish cuisine and, helped along by a few Scandi friends, came up with this take on Maksalaatikko. My rule for liver is roughly '40 seconds or 40 minutes': it has to be either flash-fried for a soft, rare dinner or cooked long and slow in a casserole to tenderize. Anything in between often fails me. This recipe is simple, creamy, sweet and delicious – but if the liver really puts you off, make it with chicken thighs instead.

Serves 6

1kg liver

1 large onion

2 fat cloves of garlic or 4 smaller ones

1 tablespoon oil, sunflower or groundnut

a fistful of rosemary or thyme or sage or 1 tablespoon dried mixed herbs

a fistful of fresh parsley

150g rice

100g sultanas

1 egg

500ml milk

¼ savoy cabbage

Rinse the livers, then cut out any green bits. Peel and chop the onion. Peel and thinly slice the garlic. Heat the oil in a large frying pan, put in the onion and garlic and cook over a medium heat for 8–10 minutes until they have softened.

Meanwhile, strip the leaves from the rosemary, thyme or sage and chop them – you need enough to fill 1 tablespoon. Chop the parsley, again enough to fill 1 tablespoon.

Add the livers to the pan. When they are sealed on all sides, throw in the rice, sultanas, your chosen herb or the mixed dried herbs and the parsley, and stir well.

Whisk together the egg and milk, and pour over the top. Bring to the boil, then turn down the heat and simmer, stirring occasionally, for 20 minutes.

Meanwhile, slice the cabbage thinly.

Check that the rice is cooked, then add the cabbage and continue to simmer until the cabbage has softened. If it shows signs of drying out, add a little water, but the finished dish should not be too wet.

Serve with a generous dollop of cranberry sauce.

CHRISTMAS FOODIE GIFT IDEAS

Peanut and chocolate chip cookie jar

This cookie jar can be adapted to suit your tastes, or the tastes of the person who you're giving it to. I've plumped for peanut and chocolate chip cookies, but try a fistful of Smarties for a present for young bakers, or some grown-up white chocolate and lemon zest, or let your imagination run wild.

makes 1 large jar

a large pretty jar
300g plain flour
150g sugar
50g milk chocolate, roughly chopped
50g dark chocolate, roughly chopped
2 fistfuls of peanuts, roughly chopped

When you've put the (incredibly cheap) ingredients into a pretty jar, add a set of handmade instructions: 'To make this cookie jar into cookies, preheat oven to 180°C/350°f/gas 4. Add 150g softened butter and one beaten egg, and mix well to combine. Roll out on a lightly floured surface to 1cm thick, cut out with a cookie cutter and place on a greased baking tray. Bake in the centre of the oven for 10–12 minutes or until golden. Leave to set for a few minutes before you dive in.'

Chilli vodka

My friend Jack made me some chilli vodka one year, and I've never forgotten it. It sat in the door of my fridge for a long time, and eventually ended up in summery ice-cold Bloody Marys, in place of the vodka and tabasco. Home-infused booze with an element of a dare – what's not to love?

makes 2 bottles

8 small fresh red chillies (the smaller they are, the hotter they are!)
4 tablespoons caster sugar
1 litre vodka
2 clean 500ml bottles

Prick the chillies all over with a pin or a small, sharp knife to release the flavour – if you dice or slice them you run the risk of pouring tiny bits of chilli into your drink! Pop 4 into each bottle, with 2 tablespoons sugar in each. Pour over the vodka, seal and shake gently to dissolve the sugar. Store in the fridge until ready to use.

St Clement's chicken Serves 4

I named this one St Clement's chicken after the old nursery rhyme, 'Oranges and lemons, sang the bells of St Clement's . . .' Although I use mandarins in mine, a mere technicality . . .

1 x whole chicken • zest of 1 lemon • 1 x 200g tin of mandarins • 75g butter (softened) • 2 sprigs fresh thyme or 1 teaspoon mixed dried herbs • a fistful of flat-leaf parsley

First, preheat your oven to 190°C. Then weigh your whole chicken to calculate the cooking time. You need to cook it for 20 minutes per 450g, plus an extra 20 minutes at the end. For example, a 1.4kg bird will need just over an hour and 20 minutes in the oven.

Grate the lemon zest into the bowl and combine it with the drained mandarins, using a fork to break up the segments. Stir in most of the butter and add the chopped thyme or mixed dried herbs and the chopped parsley.

Lift the skin from the neck of the bird and slide your fingers under the skin on the breast. Massage the butter evenly under the skin to coat the meat, then push the skin back down.

Place the chicken in a large roasting tin and brush any extra mandarin juice over the bird. Season and loosely cover with foil.

Cook according to the weight of your bird.

To check when it is ready, skewer the thickest part of the bird and the juices should run clear. Leave to rest before serving.

Pinwheel biscuits

Continuing my Finnish Christmas-dinner theme last year, I made these adorable little pinwheel biscuits, which look fancy but are very easy to prepare. They are often made with prune jam in Finland, but I used sultanas.

Makes 8

100g sultanas or prunes or 50g of each

2 tablespoons marmalade or honey

100g butter, plus extra for greasing

200g flour, plus extra for the worktop

2 teaspoons cinnamon

icing sugar, to serve

Preheat the oven to 180°C/350°F/gas 4.

Pop the fruit into a saucepan with the marmalade or honey and enough water to come halfway up the fruit. Bring to the boil, then reduce to a simmer and leave it to stew while you make easy pastry.

Grease or line a baking tray. Melt and stir the butter. Add it to the flour with the cinnamon and stir until it has a breadcrumb texture. Then add cold water, 1 tablespoon at a time, mixing with a knife until it gathers itself into a dough. It should hold together, but not be sticky. If it does become sticky, pat a handful of flour around it.

Flour the worktop, then knead the dough lightly for a couple of minutes. Break it in half, and roll out to around 3mm thick. Cut into squares – mine were 8 x 8cm. Transfer the squares to the baking tray, leaving 0.5cm spaces between them. Drain the excess liquid from the fruit. Dollop a teaspoon of stewed fruit in the centre of each square. Then cut from the corner to the centre, stopping at the fruit. Fold every other corner into the centre, for your pinwheel, pinching the last two together into the centre.

Bake in the centre of the oven for 18 minutes. Remove from the oven and leave to stand for 2 minutes. Then take them off the baking tray, before they have time to stick.

Before serving, dust with icing sugar.

TIPS: If you like a nice glaze, brush with a beaten egg before you put them into the oven. You can experiment with fillings – orange and sultana is my favourite, but prune and honey is delicious too. Leftover cranberry sauce mixed with a little marmalade would work nicely – it would also cut down on the cooking time.

Boxing Day pasties

Make something other than turkey sandwiches this year! A Boxing Day pasty is the ideal place to smuggle leftover sprouts and veg, along with any scraps of meat, gravy and cranberry sauce that might be kicking about. It's a roast dinner in a pasty. What could be better?

Serves 4

For the pastry:
125g butter, plus extra for greasing, etc.

125g lard

500g plain flour, plus extra for dusting, etc.

1 egg

For the filling:
Any quantity of leftovers from the following:

carrots, parsnips, cauliflower cheese, broccoli, other veg, turkey, chicken, ham, pigs in blankets, gravy, cranberry sauce, apple sauce, stuffing . . .

Preheat the oven to 180°C/350°F/gas 4.

First make the pastry. Dice the butter and lard. Tip the flour into a large mixing bowl and add the butter and lard. Rub into the flour with your fingertips to a breadcrumb texture, then add cold water, 1 tablespoon at a time, and mix with a knife to form a dough.

Divide the dough into 4 pieces, cover and chill for 15 minutes.

Meanwhile, take your solid leftovers and mash them roughly together in a large bowl. Add a little wetness – either gravy, cranberry sauce, apple sauce or a little stock. You don't want a slushy mixture that will leak through your pastry, but you do want a pleasantly moist one.

Lightly grease a baking tray. Lightly flour your work surface. Remove the pastry from the fridge and roll out one piece to just shy of 1cm thick. Lay a large side plate on top and cut around it with a blunt knife to form a round shape. Place a few tablespoons of the leftovers mixture in the centre. Carefully lift each side so they meet in the middle, and pinch together with your fingertips. Pinch and fold the sides in, and place on the baking tray. Repeat until all the dough and leftovers are used up.

Beat the egg and brush it over the pastry, or use your fingers if you don't have a pastry brush. Bake in the centre of the oven for 45 minutes until golden. Allow to cool for a few minutes before serving. Can be enjoyed hot or cold.

JAN | FEB
05

cabbages | mushrooms

A new year, and all change, as I moved from Southend-on-Sea to London, with the Small Boy, the cat, the guinea pig and three very important goldfish. I made marmalade (see page 170), was seduced with mushrooms on toast (page 172), and popped up on the front cover of the *Observer Food Monthly* magazine, wielding a rolling pin in a Rosie the Riveter fashion, and looking far more fierce than I really am. I was also in a six-week Sainsbury's TV advert, making a chicken curry with some leftovers from a Sunday roast as part of their Make Your Roast Go Further campaign. Life was starting to get seriously surreal...

Also in this chapter: Tanzania • Burns Night • Valentine's Day • Pancake Day

TANZANIA

I have been involved with Oxfam since I featured in their Walking the Breadline report in May 2013, and wanted to see how else I could help.

I was invited to Tanzania to visit some projects centred around women, motherhood, farming and land, and to see some of the challenges women faced elsewhere in the world.

Poverty in the UK and poverty in Africa are incomparable on so many levels, but at the core are common themes: the scapegoating and victim blaming; the attitude that if you're poor, it's somehow your own fault; the lack of representation at government level, with no parliamentarians willing to align themselves with the poor, whom they do not really understand; the inability to meet basic needs, such as food and water; the difficulty in providing for children when you have very little.

I met women who had made a change in their lives and their communities, who had stood up and been counted, who had broken traditions and political barriers. I went as part journalist, part food writer, part charity campaigner, and met Sister Martha, a former nun who had reclaimed a piece of swamp land and used it to grow fruit and vegetables. Now she runs a large farm, teaching other people to do the same. I met Maria, a young single mother who sells fish, and Irene, whose Dagaa recipe is opposite.

We may be almost five thousand miles from one another, but our basic needs and rights are the same: food, water, education for our children, an income, safe and secure housing; the right to live without fear of exploitation, financial, sexual or otherwise; the right to live without fear of abuse or violence; the right to live independently rather than with an abusive partner; to be able to give birth safely; to be treated by a doctor if you or your family fall sick.

To find out more about Oxfam's work in Tanzania, the UK, or elsewhere, please visit www.oxfam.gb or follow @OxfamGB on Twitter.

Dagaa   Serves 2

When I visited Tanzania, I came across dagaa (tiny fried fish) in almost every household I visited. We'd often eat them with stewed greens, home-ground peanut butter and ugali (soft maize), served in small bowls, with our fingers. Here is my British take on it, using sprats, which are available quite cheaply.

150g rice • 2 tablespoons oil, sunflower or groundnut • 200g sprats • 1 lime or 1 tablespoon bottled lime juice • a thumb of fresh ginger • ½ teaspoon salt • 100g spinach or spring greens • 1 tablespoon peanut butter • 1 fresh chilli

Bring a saucepan of water to the boil. Add the rice and reduce to a simmer for 20 minutes, or until cooked.

Heat the oil in a shallow frying pan, add the sprats, then squeeze or pour over the lime juice. Grate 1 teaspoon of the ginger. Add it to the pan with the salt and fry until the fish begin to crisp round the edges (no more than 10 minutes).

When the fish are almost done, blanch the greens in boiling water, put them into a bowl and stir in the peanut butter. Chop the chilli and sprinkle it over the top. Serve the fish and rice with the greens.

Sister Martha's 'just chicken' chicken soup

While I was in Tanzania, I visited last year's winner of Oxfam's Female Food Heroes competition – an Africa-wide search to celebrate female farmers and food producers who were making a difference to the lives of their communities. While we were at her house, I ate very little, having spent the night before being horrendously ill. She shook her head at the state of me, and spooned out a small bowl of clear broth, and two chicken legs, and handed it to me. 'Soupo,' she said. It turned out to be exactly what I needed, full-flavoured and slightly salty, with meltingly soft chicken falling from the bones. I devoured it, and seconds, and asked her what was in it. Sister Martha laughed.

'Kuku.'

'What else?'

'No. Just kuku.'

Just chicken, slowly stewed in its own juices – I jotted down a reminder to myself to make some when I got home. Back in the UK, still unwell and with the typical empty fridge of the returned traveller, I dug out a packet of chicken from the freezer, defrosted it and made myself 'just kuku'.

Serves 2

1 scant tablespoon oil, sunflower or groundnut

4 pieces of chicken on the bone

300ml water

a pinch of salt

lemon juice (optional)

black pepper (optional)

Place the chicken and oil in a saucepan over a medium heat. Sprinkle with a little salt and cook for 5 minutes on each side to seal. Pour over the water and turn up the heat to bring to the boil. Boil for a few minutes, then turn the heat down low and cover the pan. Simmer gently for 3 hours, or longer, until the broth is golden and the chicken very tender.

For a clearer broth, strain the liquid. Serve on its own, or with bread, a squeeze of lemon and a grinding of black pepper.

TIP: You can adapt this soup to taste. I recommend frying 2 sliced garlic cloves and a finely chopped onion with the chicken in the first stage for a heady, sweet soup with extra antioxidants. Maybe garnish with a little coriander or parsley if you have any to hand. Use it as a simple, foolproof base.

mince and rice mixture

cabbage leaves

stuff the cabbage leaves

roll the leaves up

yoghurt dip

Stuffed cabbage leaves

This is my take on Greek dolmades. I first had stuffed vine leaves at my grandad's guesthouse in Southend, and deeply regret not pilfering his recipe before he passed away. I stuff cabbage leaves, vine leaves being relatively hard to come by in comparison, which will no doubt have him swearing at me from beyond the grave, but they go down well in my house. They remind me of summers sitting at a Formica table, watching him deftly roll these delicate parcels, wiping his big worn hands on his boiler suit.

Makes around 20

1 large savoy cabbage

100g rice

1 onion

2 fat cloves of garlic, or 4 smaller ones

a fistful of parsley

a fistful of mint

1 tablespoon oil, sunflower or groundnut

400g minced meat (pork or lamb is best but turkey is good too)

a pinch of cinnamon

140g tomato purée

Remove the leaves from the cabbage and simmer them in a saucepan of boiling water for a few minutes. When they've softened, take them out with a slotted spoon and leave them to dry on a clean tea-towel or some kitchen roll.

Bring the water back to the boil, add the rice and cook for 15 minutes, or until soft and fluffy.

Peel and finely chop the onion and garlic. Chop the parsley and mint, discarding any tough stalks.

In a separate pan, heat the oil and add the onion, garlic and mince. Cook until the onion has softened and the mince has browned. Mix in the rice, parsley, mint, cinnamon and tomato purée and cook for another minute or two.

To stuff the leaves, lay a cabbage leaf on a board or work surface, place 2 teaspoons of the rice and mince mixture in the centre, fold in the sides and roll up tightly.

Eat them hot with a yoghurt, mint and cucumber dip, or cold with a squeeze of lemon.

TIP: For a more substantial main dish, put the stuffed leaves seam-side down into a roasting tin or casserole dish, pour over a tin of chopped tomatoes or 400ml chicken stock, with a few tablespoons of tomato purée stirred in, and bake in the oven at 180°C/350°F/gas 4 for 30 minutes.

Savoy cabbage, butter bean and bacon casserole

Inspired loosely, extremely loosely, by a cross between a French cassoulet and an Italian ribollita, this dish came from a variety of things in the bottom of my fridge – why change the habit of a lifetime?

Serves 4

100g dried butter beans

1 tablespoon oil

4 chicken drumsticks or thighs

1 onion

4 fat cloves of garlic or 8 smaller ones

1 carrot

100g streaky bacon

½ savoy cabbage

1 teaspoon mixed dried herbs

300ml chicken stock

1 tablespoon tomato purée

The night before you want to make this, cover the butter beans with cold water and leave them to soak for at least 8 hours. The next day, drain and rinse them thoroughly, and pop them into a saucepan. Cover with water and boil rapidly for 10 minutes, then remove from the heat.

Put the oil into a large saucepan or frying pan and add the chicken, skin-side down. Brown it over a high heat for 10 minutes, turning halfway through. Peel and chop the onion and garlic. Chop the carrot and slice the bacon into strips. Discard any tough outer leaves and the stalk from the cabbage, then slice it thinly. Add the onion, garlic, carrot and bacon with the mixed herbs to the pan, and reduce the heat to medium for a further 10 minutes, until the vegetables have softened.

Drain the butter beans and drop them into the pan with the cabbage, pour over the stock, and stir in the tomato purée. Bring to the boil, reduce to a simmer, and cover with a lid, plate or foil. Leave to cook for a further 20 minutes until the chicken is done and the sauce has thickened.

TIP: This is a dish that improves with time, so you could make it in advance and allow it to cool for the heady flavours to develop, heating it through again to serve.

BURNS NIGHT

Cock-a-leekie soup

The opening glory for Burns Night suppers in years gone by, this soup has been tweaked and reinvented many times – and will probably be a little different from this version next time I make it. It's not a looker, but it's certainly delicious. The prunes are fairly traditional, but if you don't like them, you can replace them with sultanas for a similar sweet, fruity flavour.

Serves 6

25g butter
4 boneless chicken thighs
1 onion
1 sprig of thyme
800ml chicken stock
1 large leek
100g prunes, dried or tinned
2 generous fistfuls of parsley
salt and pepper

Pop the butter into a large, heavy-based pan over a medium heat and let it melt. Lay the chicken in the melted butter, skin-side down. Cook for 4–5 minutes on each side until it has turned golden.

Peel and finely slice the onion, then add to the pan and let it soften, stirring from time to time, for about 10 minutes. Add the thyme, pour in the stock and bring to a vigorous boil for a minute or two, then reduce to a simmer for 30 minutes or until the chicken is cooked and very tender.

Trim and finely slice the leek – the white and green parts – then toss into the soup with the prunes. Cook for 5 minutes until the leeks have softened slightly.

Chop the parsley, discarding any thick stalks and stir it through the soup. Taste, season, then serve.

Home-made haggis pots with neeps and tatties Serves 4–6

On Burns Nights gone by, I introduced my friends to the concept of haggis with this cross between a haggis and a faggot (those lumps of goodness-knows-what swimming in gravy, a school dinner I remember well from the 1990s, usually served with boiled potatoes and cabbage). Not a sheep's stomach in sight, but enough offal to satisfy a Burns Night tradition. You can find sheeps' hearts extremely cheaply at your local butcher and in some supermarkets.

2 onions • 2 sheeps' hearts • 400g liver – lamb is best but chicken is fine • 50g oats • 75g shredded suet or butter, plus extra for greasing • 2 tablespoons chopped fresh sage, or 1 rounded tablespoon dried mixed herbs • a scant ½ teaspoon of cinnamon • a generous grinding of black pepper and a generous pinch of salt

Preheat the oven to 180°C/350°F/gas 4. Peel and finely chop the onions. Dice the hearts and the liver, removing any tubes or gristly bits. Pop them into a saucepan with the onions, cover with water, and bring to a vigorous boil. Cover, reduce to a simmer, and cook for 20 minutes until the onions are soft and the meat is tender. Scoop out 100ml of the cooking water and reserve it for later. Drain the rest.

Tip the meat and onions back into the saucepan and mash vigorously – or tip everything into a blender, pulse, then return it to the pan. Stir in the oats, the suet or butter, sage or mixed dried herbs and the cinnamon, with a little of the reserved cooking liquid, the salt and the pepper. Grease 6 muffin tins or a shallow roasting tin. Spoon the mixture into the muffin tins or the roasting tin, smoothing the top. Bake in the centre of the oven for 25 minutes or until firm.

Not being remotely Scottish, I've no qualms about making my neeps and tatties with either swede, turnip or baby turnips, or even parsnips if I'm desperate, but tradition dictates that they should be made with swede. If you don't fancy tackling that big hard knobbly vegetable, though, try it with baby turnips instead. Break the rules. I dare you.

4 large white potatoes • a splash of oil • salt and pepper • 1 swede • 30g butter for mashing

Preheat the oven to 180°C/350°F/gas 4. Bring a large pan of water to the boil.

Peel and halve the potatoes and pop into the boiling water for 5 minutes. Remove with a slotted spoon, put into a roasting tin, then turn off the saucepan of water – you'll need it later for the swede. Drizzle a little oil over the potatoes, season, then roast for 45 minutes until crisp. Meanwhile, peel and dice the swede, then carefully drop it into the saucepan of water. Return to the boil, and reduce to a simmer for 45 minutes, until very soft. Remove the potatoes from the oven, drain the swede, and mash the two together roughly with the butter. Season again, and serve immediately.

Tipsy laird   Serves 4–6

When I used to host Burns Night suppers, my Tipsy Laird was the stuff of legend. I later learned, looking at other people's recipes, that I was possibly rather . . . generous with the whisky. I've pared it back for this recipe, but you might want to taste as you go – the alcohol flavour deepens as you leave it in the fridge to chill!

300g sponge cake • 100ml whisky • 300g raspberries, fresh or frozen • 500ml custard • 500ml double cream • a generous fistful of flaked almonds

Cut the sponge cake into chunks and use it to line the bottom of your bowl, or each glass or bowl, if making individual portions. Pour over the whisky and scatter on the raspberries, pressing them down gently with your fingers. Keep a few raspberries to one side to decorate the top.

Pour a thick layer of custard over the raspberries, and smooth with the back of a spoon. Whip the cream to form soft peaks (an electric mixer is useful, but if you don't have one, it's a few minutes' work) and spoon it over the custard.

Top with the reserved raspberries and almonds, and chill to serve.

LOVE
IS ALL
YOU
NEED

VALENTINE'S DAY

Valentine soup

If, like me, you buy your onions by the large bag instead of individually, you might be familiar with the veg-drawer-full-of-onions scenario that I face every now and again. In this situation, a good onion soup recipe is extremely handy to have. I called this one Valentine Soup, after one of my favourite poems by Poet Laureate Carol Ann Duffy, because I'd rather have an onion than a red rose or a satin heart any day of the week.

Serves 2

2 large onions
2 fat cloves of garlic
25g butter
1 teaspoon sugar
100ml white wine
1 potato
500ml chicken stock
4 prunes, dried or tinned
100ml cream
salt and pepper
a fistful of parsley, to garnish

Peel and slice the onions very thinly. Peel and finely chop the garlic. Pop the butter into a medium saucepan. Drop in the onions and garlic, and cook slowly over a low heat until they have softened, for 10–12 minutes. The trick to good onion soup (and Valentine Soup should be no less than remarkable) is to sweat the onions slowly until they are tenderly translucent. Do not be tempted to rush this step: burned onions will ruin everything.

When the onions are translucent, stir in the sugar to dissolve, and pour over the wine. Peel and dice the potato and add to the pan. Crank the heat up to cook off the wine, then pour over the stock. Bring to the boil, then reduce to a simmer for at least 20 minutes, 30 if you can spare the time, to soften the potato.

Chop the prunes finely.

Blitz two-thirds of the soup in a blender – including all of the chunks of potato if you can find them – with the cream, then pour back into the pan with the remaining soup to warm through gently. Taste, and season.

Divide between two bowls, scatter over the prunes and chopped parsley to garnish, and finish with a twist of black pepper.

Headrush spaghetti

I called this 'headrush spaghetti', because that was exactly what happened when I tried it. The pungent intensity of the dried mushrooms, the garlic hit, and the lingering sweetness of the white chocolate . . . oh, my! It was eleven a.m. on Valentine's Day when I first knocked it together, and I gobbled the lot as I typed the recipe on to my blog, eager to share it with my readers so they could have a delicious bowl of it for themselves. This recipe is not just for Valentine's Day, but that's a pretty good place to start.

Serves 2

200g spaghetti
200g mushrooms, dried
4 fat cloves of garlic, or 6–8 smaller ones
2 tablespoons oil, sunflower or groundnut, or butter
40g white chocolate
100ml cream
a fistful of fresh parsley
50g hard, strong cheese

Pop a pan of water on to boil. Put in the pasta and cook according to the packet instructions, for around 8–10 minutes.

To make the sauce, pound the mushrooms to break them down. If you don't have a mortar and pestle, use a pair of kitchen scissors and a teacup, or a rolling pin or an empty bottle on a chopping board or work surface. Or fling them into a blender. Just do what you have to do to crush them a bit. Put them into a small bowl, cover them with water and leave to rehydrate (about 30 minutes).

Cheat-roast the garlic: pop it into a bowl or on to a saucer, rub a little oil into the papery skins, and put it into the microwave on a high heat for 30 seconds. Grate the white chocolate. When the mushrooms have rehydrated, drain them, then squash the sweet garlic pulp from the skins into the dried mushrooms and stir in the cream and white chocolate. Add a dash of the spaghetti water and warm the sauce through. Toss it into the spaghetti with the oil or butter. Tear or chop the parsley, grate the cheese and scatter over the top.

TIPS: Drying mushrooms deeply intensifies their flavour. I buy fresh ones from the reduced chiller at the supermarket when I find them – all varieties – and pop them on a baking sheet in the oven for 40 minutes at 180°C/350°F/gas 4 until they're crisp. They should snap like a cracker when cool.

When your mushrooms have dried out, allow them to cool, then store them in a clean airtight jar. I've had mine for around 6 months now in a Kilner jar, and they're still good.

Bolognon   Serves 2

Faced with a leftover hunk of beef to stretch between two grown women with fairly healthy appetites, I started making a bolognese, changed my mind and wanted bourguignon, and changed it back halfway through. This was the first dinner I cooked for Someone Very Special (who had cooked for me the evening before, hence the leftover beef!). Cue one mild flap about what to do and subsequent messing about with it at every stage. The result, however, is a chunky, obscenely rich, heady, delicious big butch dinner that I've christened Bolognon, in honour of its roots. And, God, it's good. She thought so too.

2 onions (told you, I'm stretching this one out) • 2 fat cloves of garlic, or 3–4 smaller ones • 1 carrot • 2 tablespoons oil or a knob of butter • 250g beef • 150g bacon – smoked streaky is good • a few sprigs of thyme and rosemary • 100ml milk • 1 x 400g tin of chopped tomatoes • 200ml red wine • 4 tablespoons tomato purée, dissolved in 400ml chicken, beef or vegetable stock • a huge fistful of parsley • 150g spaghetti or a chunky pasta variety • 2 tablespoons double cream or 1 rounded tablespoon natural yoghurt with 2 teaspoons sugar • 50g hard, strong cheese (optional) • black pepper (optional)

Peel and finely slice the onions. Peel and chop the garlic, and grate the carrot. Heat the oil or butter in a large frying pan or heavy-bottomed casserole dish, then add the onions and garlic. Cook over a low heat for 8–10 minutes until the onions have softened.

Meanwhile, finely slice the beef, chop the bacon, and add them to the pan. Turn up the heat to seal the meat, stirring to ensure it doesn't stick to the bottom of the pan. Pick enough leaves from the thyme and rosemary to fill 2 teaspoons. Pour in the milk and stir well – it will turn brown with the meat juices and softened onions so don't panic! Pour over the tomatoes, wine, tomato purée and stock, toss in the chopped herbs and stir well. Crank the heat right up to bring it to the boil.

Cover the pan with foil/a plate/a lid and leave on a very low heat for 1 hour, after which the beef will be 'soft enough'. (As I was going all out to impress, I cooked mine for 4 hours. The beef was meltingly soft and the sauce thick and rich.) For a cheaper version, bring it to a furious boil, cover the pan tightly and turn off the heat. Leave it to stand for 1 hour, bring to the boil again and repeat. The covered pan will retain the heat and continue to cook the bolognon, without a constant supply of gas or electricity.

Cook the spaghetti or chunky pasta according to the packet instructions, around 8–10 minutes, shortly before the bolognon is ready.

Stir the cream or yoghurt-and-sugar through the bolognon just before you serve. Dollop atop a heap of spaghetti or chunky pasta to complement the tender beef and thick sauce . . . As I was going for full-on punchy knock-your-socks-off delicious, I tossed handfuls of cheese over it, and a good grinding of pepper to finish up.

Love marmalade

This was a labour of love, hence the name, but of the sticky, delicious variety. We talked about it for a week, eventually got around to halving, gutting and slicing the oranges, left them on the doorstep all day, disappeared off to a seventieth birthday party in the country, and eventually bottled it at half past two in the morning. I recommend you set aside some time to make it all in one hit, and enjoy yourself . . .

Makes about 6 jars

a piece of muslin or a clean tea-towel

1kg oranges, Seville if available

zest and juice of 2 lemons or 4 tablespoons bottled lemon juice

2kg any sugar or a mixture of any, except icing sugar

a good slosh of whisky

clean jars

waxed or greaseproof paper, cut into circles to fit inside the jars

First, grab your marmalade-making pan – it needs to be a fairly big one, stock-pot-sized, to allow for a serious quantity of marmalade and some vigorous bubbling up the sides. Place the muslin or the tea-towel over the top of the pan.

Put a couple of saucers into the fridge or freezer: you'll need them for testing the set of your marmalade later on.

Wash the oranges and lemons. Pick out the green stalks and discard. Halve the fruit, then squeeze the juice into the pan through the cloth. Push your fingers inside them to get those juices out, then grab a spoon. Allegra recommends 'a shallow-bowled dessert spoon – you're going to use it for digging, so preferably one with a slightly pointy end'. Use the spoon to dig out all the pith, pulp and membrane, and spoon it into the cloth. Repeat with all of the oranges and lemons.

When the fruit is stripped out, twist the cloth up tight and tie it to the pan handle. If your pan doesn't have a handle, rest it gently in the bottom of the pan. Tie the ends of the cloth around a wooden spoon and balance it on the outer edge of the pan.

Slice the lemon and orange rind into matchstick-thin pieces, using a really sharp knife, and pop them into the pan. Pour over 2.5 litres of water and place on a high heat on the biggest ring of your hob. Make sure the ends of the cloth bag are hanging out of the pan so they don't get immersed in boiling hot liquid: you'll need to handle them later.

Bring to the boil, then reduce to a vigorous simmer. You're aiming to reduce the quantity by around a third in 2 hours, so if it starts to come down too quickly, or doesn't look like it's moving, adjust the heat accordingly. Don't be tempted to rush this step: once you add the sugar, the chopped rind will harden, so it needs to be soft and tender before you do so.

When the liquid has reduced, lift out the cloth bag. Using a slotted spoon, squeeze, squeeze, squeeze it, scraping the jelly that oozes out of the bag back into the pan. This took me a good 10 minutes, but the jelly contains the pectin that will set the marmalade, so keep at it. It's extremely satisfying. I ended up using my hands once it had cooled a little, squeezing, twisting and scraping. Do whatever works for you, but keep going until it's got nothing left to give you.

Pour in the sugar and a good slosh of whisky, then stir slowly until the sugar has dissolved. Bring to the boil and, as it starts to climb up the sides of the pan, hold it there for a good 20 minutes, stirring to disturb the pieces of orange and lemon rind at the bottom of the pan.

Heat the oven to 140°C/275°F/gas 1, unscrew the lids from the jars, and pop them all in for around 15 minutes.

When the marmalade has boiled for 20 minutes, grab one of your cold saucers and drop a teaspoon of marmalade on to it. Leave it to cool for half a minute, then give it a prod with your finger. If it wrinkles slightly and sticks to your finger, it's ready to come off the heat. If it doesn't, reduce the marmalade to a vigorous simmer for another 10 minutes and try again. Oranges, lemons and sugar are not created equal, so there's no telling how long this step will take. It can be anything up to 30 minutes, so be patient and keep testing every few minutes.

When you have a wrinkled sticky drop of marmalade on your saucer, remove the pan from the heat, and allow it to cool for around 20 minutes, skimming the surface as it cools to get rid of any scummy bits.

Ladle the marmalade into a jug, and pour it into the jars. Carefully place the wax circles on top and leave to cool with the lids off. If you have cats, guinea pigs or children, put them into the microwave as a 'safekeeping cupboard' overnight. When cool, screw the lids on, and label them accordingly.

First-date mushrooms on toast

There's a story that goes, once upon a time I went on a date with a woman and she gave me mushrooms on toast for dinner and front-door keys for breakfast. So, although you might not associate the humble mushroom on toast with knock-your-pants-off seduction, I certainly do. If you want your own happy ending, give this a go. I can't make any promises on the romance front, but if the worst comes to the worst and you don't get a goodnight kiss, well, you'll still have had a stunningly good, simple supper.

Serves 2

1 onion

2 fat cloves of garlic

1 sprig of thyme, or 1 scant teaspoon mixed dried herbs

25g butter

300g mushrooms

a splash of red or white wine

4 thick slices of bread

100g cream cheese

salt and pepper to season

a generous fistful of leaves – spinach, rocket, something green

a drizzle of oil

a squeeze of lemon juice

Peel and slice the onion. Peel and finely chop the garlic. Pick the thyme leaves, if using. Toss all three into a frying pan with the butter. Cook for about 10 minutes over a low heat until the onion has softened. Chop the mushrooms rough and chunky, and add to the pan with the wine. Crank up the heat and continue to cook, stirring occasionally.

Meanwhile, toast the bread – your mushrooms are nearly done!

When the toast is ready, pop it on to the plates. Stir the cream cheese into the mushrooms and season well, then spoon on to the toast. Garnish with some leaves on the side, a drizzle of oil, a squish of lemon – and enjoy.

Come-to-bed carbonara

Rich but delicate, heady and involving, with sweet soft garlic, the salty tang of bacon and a buttery, creamy sauce. If you're cooking this with the intention to impress someone special (and I certainly was), put on some Billie Holiday, Peggy Lee or Ella Fitzgerald, low, slow and crooning. Pour yourself a glass of wine, relax and focus. Put the scales away, quantities are approximate, and enjoy yourself . . .

Serves 2

4 fat cloves of garlic, or 6 smaller ones

100g streaky bacon

1 sprig of rosemary

20g butter

100ml white wine

160g spaghetti

4 eggs

100ml cream

a fistful of spinach

50g hard, strong cheese, to serve

a generous grinding of black pepper

Peel and finely chop the garlic. Chop the bacon. Strip the rosemary leaves from the stalk and chop them too. Put the garlic, bacon and rosemary with the butter into a medium saucepan over a low heat. Add half of the wine, stir in slowly as the butter melts, then add the rest and stir again.

Bring a pan of water to the boil, add the spaghetti and cook according to the packet instructions, usually for 8–10 minutes.

Separate the eggs and reserve the whites for future use – either make meringues with them for dessert (see page 70) or an egg-white omelette for breakfast after such an indulgent dinner! Drop the yolks into the sauce and beat in quickly. Remove from the heat to prevent the sauce splitting and stir in the cream.

Before serving, drop the spinach into the pasta water to wilt it. Drain and rinse the spaghetti and spinach together. Tip back into the pan, toss with the sauce and split between two bowls. Scatter over the cheese and grind over some pepper. Dig in!

TIP: If the sauce does split, all is not lost! Put it to one side, and make a quick roux with a knob of butter and 1 rounded teaspoon of flour in a pan over a low heat. Add a splash of water or milk and mix to make a rough paste. Add a splash of the carbonara sauce, stir until smooth, and repeat until all of the sauce is incorporated. Rescued!

PANCAKE DAY

Silver-dollar pancakes

Makes around 20 tiny pancakes, serves around 4

200g plain flour

1 tablespoon baking powder

1 tablespoon sugar

a pinch of salt

2 eggs

300ml milk

30g melted butter, plus extra for frying

200g streaky bacon

6 tablespoons maple syrup

I first came across silver-dollar pancakes on the brunch menu at Blackfoot in London's Exmouth Market: tiny American pancakes served with melon and yoghurt, or bacon and soft, spiced apples. I make mine with traditional maple syrup and bacon – but have them as you will.

Stir together the dry ingredients in a mixing bowl, and make a well in the centre.

Break the eggs into the well, then pour in the milk and melted butter, and stir well to combine. Cover the mixture with a tea-towel and leave to stand for 30 minutes.

Melt a little butter in a frying pan, and dollop 1 scant tablespoon of batter into the pan to make one pancake. Repeat, leaving a clear 2cm around each to allow for spreading. When the pancake is bubbling on the top, turn it over for 1 minute, then remove from the pan. You might need to do these in batches – keep them warm, separated from each other with greaseproof paper or cling film.

In a separate pan, fry the bacon until crisp. Serve alongside the pancakes with a drizzle of maple syrup!

Perfect pancakes

As a parent, I felt pancakes were one of those things I had to know how to make. I got away with it for the first few years, making squat little American pancakes and filling them with exciting flavours, like sliced apple, banana and cinnamon, a handful of sultanas. But this year my boy asked me for 'rolly-up' pancakes. Ah, I thought. That involves a degree of skill and, contrary to popular opinion, I'm not that much of a tosser. Anyway, to cut a long story short, I fiddled about with a few pancake recipes and ended up here – but I still can't do the nonchalant fling into the air and catch. There's no shame in that: I have a good wide fish slice to do the job for me.

Serves 4

100g flour
a pinch of salt
2 eggs
1 tablespoon oil, sunflower or groundnut, or melted butter, plus extra for frying
300ml milk

Tip the flour into a mixing bowl, add the salt, and stir briefly to combine.

Make a well in the centre and crack in both of the eggs. Add the oil or melted butter and half of the milk, then beat together to form a smooth if slightly thick batter. Gradually add the rest of the milk until all of it has been incorporated.

Cover and leave to rest for 30 minutes.

When the batter has rested, lightly grease a frying pan with oil or butter and warm over a medium heat.

When the fat is hot (but not burning), dollop a scant ladle of batter into the centre of the pan, and tip it about so it spreads to the edges.

Fry for a minute or so on a medium heat. Then, if you aren't an accomplished tosser, carefully lift your pancake with a fish slice or spatula and turn it over to cook the other side. Keep warm, separating the pancakes from each other with greaseproof paper or cling film, while you make the rest.

Serve warm with lemon and sugar, or chocolate spread.

Nana pancakes

What do you make for breakfast when you have a sad-looking banana, eggs, milk and flour? Nana pancakes, of course! A hit with children and adults alike in my house, and vegan versions can be made with a milk substitute (oat, rice or soya milk) and an extra banana in place of the egg.

Makes 6 good-sized pancakes

1–2 bananas
100g self-raising flour
1 egg
100ml milk
a fistful of sultanas (optional)
2 tablespoons oil

Peel and slice the bananas. Then, depending on their ripeness, either mash them with a fork or chop-chop-chop them into tiny pieces. Put them into a large mixing bowl. Add the flour and stir. Crack in the egg, pour in the milk and toss in the sultanas, then mix with a fork to form a smooth batter.

Heat the oil in a frying pan and add a tablespoon of batter. Cook over a medium heat for a minute or two on each side. Repeat until all of the batter is used up. Keep them warm, separated from each other with greaseproof paper or cling film.

Serve in a heap with lemon, sugar, honey, warmed peanut butter – whatever you've got. The choice is yours!

Busking with Billy Bragg

There's no culinary story attached to this anecdote, apart from a pint of bitter and a burger afterwards, but I've included it because this was one of the points at which I realized life had changed. I was a columnist for a national newspaper, singing outside a tube station with a man whose albums I'd been buying for years. A far cry from pulling out a mattress from underneath a single bed in a house I shared with five strangers – in those days, I couldn't even have afforded the train fare to get to Camden Town. It was one of the best parts of my year, so here you go . . .

I've sung in bands on and off over the years, but performing in public has always been a nervous, shaky and awkward affair. I had a piano and two guitars until I sold all my stuff a couple of years ago to try to catch up with rent arrears and get back on my feet – and I haven't really sung or played since. I had always wanted to try busking but found the idea daunting – especially doing it alone.

But then came a challenge I couldn't turn down: busking outside Camden tube station with Billy Bragg, one of my musical and political heroes, who was happy to tutor and coax me through a playlist we had chosen together a few days before. When he called me, I didn't answer my phone, staring at it like a lovestruck schoolgirl. Billy Bragg was on my phone. Giggle, giggle, panic, giggle. I got it together enough to call him back – and he was in Morrisons doing his weekly shop. It helped. Just a normal bloke, pottering around the supermarket. I took a deep breath and started to talk in what I hoped was a normal voice, and we worked out some songs that we both knew.

It didn't help that on the Sunday before our busking date, disaster struck: I lost my voice. How on earth was I going to be able to sing 'A New England' with any degree of competency? I took to Twitter for help, and tried everything that was suggested: hot water with honey and lemon; lashings of turmeric neat on a teaspoon; my own Feisty Soup, with garlic and ginger, chillies, lemon and tomatoes. By the time the day arrived, I was still speaking in a husky voice.

Billy and I met for a quick rehearsal and busking lesson beforehand at the Underworld in Camden. 'The Times They Are a-Changin'' by Bob Dylan was my request: it seemed fitting and, having rehearsed it to myself in the kitchen a few days before, I knew it was within my severely limited vocal range. As we left the intimate cocoon of the pub, my bouncy excitement became more of a trudge as, heart in mouth, I babbled and swore, and panicked that I couldn't do it, terrified that stage fright and nerves would overtake me, that my tentative voice would abandon me altogether.

We found a spot outside HSBC – oh, the irony – and I took a swig from a hip flask of hot water, honey and lemon, and another swig of Buttercup cough syrup before we kicked off. Billy played guitar and I shouted the words along beside him.

Standing on a corner singing, with people rushing past you, is strange. With my only recent experience of public performance being to fixated crowds at conferences, I wanted to stop them, ask them why they weren't staying to listen. It was almost as though I was giving a speech again at the People's Assembly or the Labour Party Conference and everyone had just simultaneously got up and left the room. Discombobulating. But, gradually, a crowd started to gather, and several people took out their phones to record us. Initial fear had given way to a surge of adrenalin, in response to a positive reaction from the assembled crowd. A white-van man even whipped his head round to listen while he waited at the traffic lights, as we belted out 'Oh My Sweet Carolina' into the noisy, grey streets.

We're not really used to spontaneous outbursts of singing in the UK. I spent ten days in Tanzania with Oxfam visiting food and farming projects earlier in the year, and one of the things that struck me most on the trip was the music: everywhere we went, men and women would dance and sing to welcome us to their villages. When I came back to London, the only music to be heard was an old accordion player sitting outside Marks & Spencer, trying to catch the eyes of passers-by to make a few quid.

Now it was my turn to be the busker – a queer juxtaposition of vulnerability and empowerment. I put on my performance face, threw back my head and enjoyed myself, safe in the knowledge that standing beside me was a man with decades of busking experience and a natural affinity with the crowd. Between us, and during four songs, we made just over thirty-eight pounds.

And, call me a silly romantic thing, but whisper-singing 'Can't Help Falling In Love' on a busy street corner to my beloved, is one of the most exciting things I've ever done. Even if it was in a husky croak, and I couldn't quite manage the chorus . . .

PREVIOUS PAGE:
'Standing on a corner singing, with people rushing past you, is a strange experience.'
Photograph: Linda Nylind for the *Guardian*

MAR | APR
06

rhubarb | spring herbs | spring greens

March was the month I was on the front cover of
Diva magazine, talking about politics, being an
out gay woman, food, poverty and marriage(!).
Hold the rumour mill – it was about the Equal
Marriage Act in general, not a big announcement
on my part. I also celebrated the launch of my first
book, *A Girl Called Jack*, with as many people as I
could who had helped me along the way – I'd love
to say it was a brilliant night but I don't remember
very much of it! Hic!

Smoked mackerel on toast with hot quick rhubarb salsa

Healthy, tasty and inexpensive, mackerel is one of my favourite fish. It's sublime if you can get it really fresh, but it is, of course, widely available smoked, and pairs brilliantly with the acidity of rhubarb. Try this for a speedy tasty lunch.

Serves 2–4

100g fresh rhubarb

1 fresh chilli or a pinch of dried chilli flakes

juice of 1 lime or 1 tablespoon bottled lime juice, plus extra to serve

2 teaspoons honey, plus extra to serve

300g smoked mackerel

4 slices wholemeal bread

100g fresh spinach or salad leaves

Thinly slice the rhubarb and the fresh chilli, if using. Put the rhubarb with the fresh or dried chilli, the lime juice, honey and 1 tablespoon of water into a small saucepan. Bring to the boil, put the lid on and let it simmer for about 5 minutes over a medium heat, stirring occasionally to stop it sticking to the pan. Add a splash more water if it needs loosening up.

Remove the lid and let it soften gently for another 5 minutes, until the salsa's consistency is as thick as you'd like it. Keep it hot.

Meanwhile, warm the smoked mackerel fillets under a hot grill – about 5 minutes each side. Make the toast.

Serve the mackerel flaked on the toast, alongside the salsa and spinach, with a squeeze of lime and a little honey drizzled over the top.

Rhubarb bread

I first made this bread for a food video. The original brief was soda bread, but rummaging around that morning, I found a few sad, soggy stalks of rhubarb sitting in the sink with clear instructions from my dearest to use them up in something. We'd had mackerel with a hot rhubarb salsa for lunch the day before, and this was born from the scraps and leftovers. A hit with all the film crew and friends present – I got about half a bite!

Serves 4

juice of ½ lemon

300ml any milk

350g flour, plus extra for dusting, etc.

1 rounded teaspoon bicarbonate of soda

100g fresh rhubarb (approx. 1 big stalk)

a thumb of fresh ginger

Preheat the oven to 180°C/350°F/gas 4.

Squeeze the lemon juice into the milk and leave it to stand for a few minutes to curdle and sour. If it looks a bit gross, you've done it right.

Put the flour and bicarb into a large mixing bowl and stir briefly to combine. Finely slice the rhubarb, and peel and grate 2 teaspoons of the ginger and mix them in.

Make a well in the centre of the dry ingredients and pour in most of the soured milk. Mix well to form a dough. Use your judgement – if the mixture is cracking and crumbly, add the rest of the soured milk. If it's clinging to your fingers in a sticky mess, add a couple more tablespoons of flour.

Dust a loaf tin with flour and drop in the batter. Shake from side to side gently to roughly fill the tin. Score a deep line down the centre (Irish folklore says this is to let the fairies out) and dust the top with extra flour.

Bake in the centre of the oven for 40 minutes, and leave to cool slightly before serving.

TIP: Serve sliced thick and chunky, with a smear of honey and some smoked mackerel fillet perched on top.

Rhubarb and ginger crumble

This year, I have an abundant crop of rhubarb growing on my roof, which every now and again I remember about, potter up the stairs, and harvest a bunch. I find new and inventive ways to use it up, like in breads (Rhubarb Bread, page 188) and salsas (Hot Quick Rhubarb Salsa, page 186). But sometimes traditional comfort is best, and what better than a steaming hot bowl of sweet, gingery crumble?

Serves 6

600g fresh rhubarb
6cm thumb of fresh ginger
100g sugar – I like soft dark brown sugar, but any will do
150g flour
75g porridge oats
100g butter

Preheat the oven to 180°C/350°F/gas 4.

Trim and slice the rhubarb into 1cm chunks and place in the bottom of an ovenproof dish. For best results use one around 20cm across, but it's not an absolute requirement.

Peel the ginger and grate it over the rhubarb, then sprinkle on 50g of the sugar evenly. Stir briefly to combine.

To make the crumble topping, put the flour and oats into a large mixing bowl. Dice the butter and add it to the bowl, then rub it in with your fingertips until it is all incorporated. Pour in the remaining 50g sugar and stir in.

Scatter half of the crumble topping over the rhubarb and pat it down with your finger-tips. Repeat with most of the remaining half, then sprinkle the rest loosely on top.

Bake in the centre of the oven for around 40 minutes, or until the rhubarb is soft and tender and the topping is a deliciously crunchy golden brown.

If the top starts to burn, or cook faster than the rest, take the dish out of the oven and cover it with foil. Turn the oven down a notch and continue to cook.

Jewelled clafoutis

When I was ambling through various cookbooks in my late teens and early twenties, I was always intimidated by the idea of making a clafoutis so I didn't attempt to cook one. Maybe it was the fancy name, or the expensive cherries traditionally found in this dessert, or perhaps because I didn't often have six people to make a dessert for and didn't trust myself with the whole thing in the house! Whatever the reason, I plucked up the courage a few months ago to try it, and it couldn't have been easier.

Once I'd made a traditional cherry one, I got exploring with colours and flavours, and this is definitely my favourite. The sweetness of the mandarins perfectly complements the acidity of the rhubarb, and the colours look beautiful together. If I'm feeling particularly fancy or artistic, I chuck in some blackberries or blueberries for good measure.

Serves 4–6

1 x 298g tin of mandarins
20g butter
3 tablespoons sugar, plus extra for the baking dish
50g milk
75g double cream
2 eggs
1 rounded tablespoon flour
400g rhubarb

Preheat the oven to 180°C/350°F/gas 4.

Drain the tinned mandarins and reserve the juice. Pop it into a jar and leave it in the fridge: it may come in handy as a salad dressing, or a glaze for roast meat or carrots – there's all sorts of uses for it.

Use a little of the butter to grease a baking dish. Sprinkle the inside of the dish with sugar, and shake gently to coat the sides evenly. Tip out any that doesn't stick.

Pop the remaining butter into a saucepan over a very, very low heat to melt – and watch it! Do not allow it to burn or it will be bitter and ruin your lovely dessert. When it has melted, remove the pan quickly from the heat and set to one side. Pour in the milk and cream and stir to combine.

Break the eggs into a mixing bowl, add the sugar, and whisk until pale and creamy. Spoon in the flour, whisk again until smooth, then slowly add the cream mixture from the pan. Add a little, whisk until smooth, and repeat until all the liquid is incorporated.

Slice the rhubarb thinly. Lay it with the mandarins in the bottom of the baking dish. Pour the batter over the top, and bake in the centre of the oven for 30 minutes, or until a knife inserted into the middle comes out clean.

Serve warm, with extra sugar sprinkled on top.

Lazarus pesto

This came about last spring, when I had a large black bunch of mint in the fridge, some sticky, soggy parsley and a clump of basil that had seen better days. Add to that a hard cheese rind and you can see why everyone wants to come to lunch at my gaff! I decided to whack it all in the blender and see if I could raise those sad herbs from the dead . . . And *voilà*. Lazarus pesto was born, and the guinea pig sulked a little, because he normally gets the ropy stuff. I used cheap salted cashew nuts and gave them a thorough rinse to get all the salt off – find them in the snacks or World Foods department of the supermarket rather than the baking aisle, where they will be more expensive. You can substitute peanuts, which are also cheap.

For 2 decent-sized jars

½ bunch of mint, approx. 50g

½ bunch of basil, approx. 50g

½ bunch of parsley, approx.50g

4 cloves of garlic, or 6–8 smaller ones

100g cashew nuts

zest and juice of 1 lemon

50g hard, strong cheese

100ml oil, sunflower or groundnut

Stuff the herbs into the blender – stalks and all – and pulse them to chop finely. If you don't have a blender, my favourite method of chopping herbs is to pop them into a mug and go at them with kitchen scissors – far tidier and easier than fiddling about with a knife! Put the chopped herbs into a bowl.

Peel and chop the garlic, then chop the nuts (by hand) or add them to the herbs in the blender. Grate the lemon zest and the cheese, and add to the herbs.

Squeeze over the lemon juice, pour over the oil, and either pulse or mix well. If you like your pesto a little looser, add a splash more oil or a little water.

Spoon into clean jars, and top with a thin layer of oil to keep the air out. Pop lids on, and store in the fridge for up to 1 week or the freezer for 3 months.

TIPS: You can use any herbs to make a pesto, and greens too, so don't worry if you don't have my magic three. A fresh herb like mint or basil is pretty essential, but rosemary, thyme and parsley make a good winter pesto.

Affectionately referred to as 'Laz' for the few weeks it survived in the fridge, it made a great base for a *pasta alla Genovese* with some sliced tinned potatoes and some green veg added, and for a risotto, added to the stock, with diced root veg tossed through. I splashed the dregs clinging to the edges of the jar with a little oil and white wine vinegar for a salad dressing. Not bad for some dead herbs at the back of the fridge!

Salsa verde **Serves 2**

'Green sauce' is traditionally made with capers but I tend not to have any, so substitute a kick of vinegar and a pinch of salt.

2 fat cloves of garlic or 4 smaller ones • 6 anchovy fillets • 2 large fistfuls of flat-leaf parsley • a large fistful of basil • a large fistful of mint • a few capers or a finely diced gherkin (optional) • 100ml oil • 3 tablespoons wine vinegar, red or white • 1 scant teaspoon English mustard • a pinch of salt

Finely dice everything and toss together with the oil, vinegar, mustard and salt. It's that simple. Spoon into a jar to store in the fridge for up to 3 days.

Spring veg risotto

This risotto was the result of a root around in the fridge and freezer to feed extra mouths at the table – originally christened 'b***ks rice' for its thrown-together status, and a surprise hit for its fresh, simple flavours.**

Serves 2

1 onion

2 fat cloves of garlic

2 tablespoons oil, sunflower or groundnut, plus extra to serve

150g long-grain white rice

100ml white wine

300ml chicken stock

¼ savoy cabbage

a fistful of fresh parsley

100g frozen garden peas

salt and pepper

Peel and finely slice the onion. Peel and chop the garlic. Put them into a frying pan with the oil over a medium heat and cook for 8–10 minutes until they have softened.

Add the rice and stir for 5 minutes, to stop it sticking to the bottom of the pan, until the edges are translucent.

Pour over the wine and stir until it has been absorbed. Add a splash of the chicken stock and repeat, stirring, until the rice is al dente and the liquid thick and soupy.

Discard any tough outer leaves from the cabbage, then chop it and the parsley finely. Stir them into the rice mixture with the peas. Heat through to defrost the peas. Taste, and season.

Leave to rest for 5 minutes before serving. Add a drizzle of oil to serve.

TIP: Substitute any other green veg for the green veg above (finely chopped broccoli, green beans or lettuce would work well) – let your imagination run as wild as your veg drawer will let you. Also delicious with chopped streaky bacon – but, then, I think most things can be improved with bacon!

Muffizzas

It's sort of a muffin, sort of a pizza, sort of a ridiculously named open-topped toasted-sandwich-bun thing. It was a quick late-night munchy snack after a long day and it occurred to me that it would be a fab lunchbox alternative to sandwiches, and great for fussy households or involving the kids in cooking: everyone can add what they like to theirs. Radical, I know. I used some of the Kale Pesto (see page 108) that was in the freezer, but see below for other suggestions. Pesto of any kind is optional, but utterly delicious.

Makes 12; serves 4–6 depending on appetite

6 white breakfast muffins, halved

1 x 400g tin of chopped tomatoes or 140g tomato purée

2 balls of mozzarella

2 tablespoons pesto or finely chopped basil, whole basil leaves or spinach

Halve the muffins: 1 muffin will make 2 muffizzas. Spread a dollop of chopped tomatoes on top or a little tomato purée, right to the edges. Add slices of mozzarella and a dollop of pesto to cover, then toast under the grill until the cheese is melting. *Voilà*.

TIP: Experiment with toppings: leftover chilli, anchovies or olives would be immense on these with a layer of cheese on top.

Fred

I made this for Mothers' Day – entertaining our rather modern family, with an accidental large amount of cream to get through. It's a lemon and thyme semi-freddo, but by the end of dinner and several glasses of wine, we'd affectionately named it Fred – 'Anyone for the last of Fred?' Fred was a huge success with all mothers present. If you're a bit suspicious of herbs in desserts, leave them out or substitute a fistful of chopped berries.

Serves 10

zest and juice of 2 lemons or 4 tablespoons bottled lemon juice

a fistful of thyme sprigs

6 egg yolks

100g caster sugar

500ml double cream

First, grate the zest from the lemons, if using, and pick 2 teaspoons of leaves off the thyme sprigs. Squeeze the lemons. Put the zest and thyme leaves into a small bowl. Set to one side.

Next, line a 700g loaf tin, Tupperware box or empty ice-cream tub with two layers of cling film, using your fingers to push it into the corners, with a few centimetres spare all round. This is to make the semi-freddo easy to remove later. (If you don't have any cling film, you can skip this step, but it will get a bit messy.)

Separate the eggs and refrigerate the whites – you can make meringues with them to serve alongside Fred (see page 70) or a simple egg-white omelette.

Pop the yolks into a large mixing bowl and pour in the sugar. Add two-thirds of the zest and thyme, and beat together until the yolks are pale and fluffy, and the mixture has doubled in size.

Add the cream and lemon juice, and beat well until it forms stiff peaks – I used to have to make this with a friend on hand to take turns at beating it, but I seem to be able to do it all by myself these days! If you have an electric whisk or stand mixer loitering around, now would be a great time to get it out, but if not, put some loud music on, get a rhythm going, and it'll be done before you know it.

When the mixture is light and fluffy and forms soft peaks – drops off an overturned spoon or fingers slowly – you're good to go. Scatter the remaining zest and thyme over the bottom of the loaf tin and give it a shake to disperse it over the bottom – when turned out, it will sit prettily on the top.

Carefully spoon the cream mixture into the loaf tin. Give it a gentle shake to get it into all the corners and smooth the top. Carefully fold the cling film over the top, and leave in the freezer for 4 hours or until frozen firm.

To serve, remove from the freezer, unwrap the cling film and turn out on to a plate. Carefully peel away the cling film and leave for a few minutes at room temperature to soften before slicing.

Ribollita

Serves 6

4 fat cloves of garlic

1 large onion or
2 small ones

2 carrots or
1 sweet potato

1 rounded teaspoon
fennel seeds

1 fresh red chilli or a pinch
of dried chilli flakes

2 tablespoons oil,
sunflower or groundnut

sausages, bacon,
shredded chicken, pork,
etc. (optional)

1 x 400g tin of butter
beans or other
white beans

½ glass of white wine

4 tablespoons
tomato purée

600ml chicken stock
or water

2 slices of bread

100g dried pasta

the rind of some hard,
strong cheese (optional)

a few fistfuls of greens
– kale, spring greens,
spinach

a fistful of flat-leaf parsley

salt and pepper

This dish came about one evening as a fridge-clearing exercise before we tripped off on holiday to visit friends. Facing a pile of cooked pasta, kale, one sausage, one rasher of bacon and a bit of pork left over from Sunday, I decided to muck about with a ribollita, and this was the result. If you don't have any scrappy odds and sods of meat lying around, this makes a delicious vegetarian or vegan version. The ingredients are approximate – use what you have instead of worrying about weighing your spring greens. I keep the rind from a wedge of hard, strong cheese to toss into dishes like this one, fishing it out before serving to avoid giving anyone a hard, strong surprise! This dish will keep in the fridge for a day or two, continuing to improve, so don't be afraid to make a big batch.

Peel and roughly chop the garlic. Peel and finely slice the onion. Dice the carrot or peel and dice the sweet potato. Toss all three into a large heavy-based pan or casserole dish – you can finish this in the oven, if you like, but I prefer to stir it on the stove with a watchful eye.

Add the fennel seeds, chopped chilli and oil, and cook over a low heat for 10 minutes or until the onions are translucent. If you're adding meat, cook it now, if necessary. Then chop it up and toss it into the pan.

Drain and rinse the beans, then tip them in. Pour over the wine, crank up the heat and cook for 5 minutes. Now stir in the tomato purée and stock, and boil vigorously for a minute or two, then reduce to a simmer.

Tear up the bread and fling it in with the pasta and cheese rind, if using, and simmer for 30 minutes to 1 hour, depending on your available time, patience and how keen an eye you keep on your gas or electricity bill! Toss in the greens and chopped parsley 15 minutes before the end.

Taste, and season before serving.

Spring herb pasta

This recipe is a great place to put any herbs you need to use up and is easy to adapt, depending on what you have available. Use at least one herb with a nice fresh flavour, like mint, basil or coriander, but pad it out with something milder, like good old flat-leaf parsley.

Serves 2

160g chunky pasta, like penne

2 generous fistfuls of mixed spring herbs

½ lettuce or 100g spring greens

50g strong, hard cheese

1 tablespoon butter

black pepper

First, pop a pan of water on for the pasta. When the water is boiling, add the pasta and cook according to the packet instructions, for usually around 8–10 minutes. While it's cooking, finely chop your herbs, including the stalks (not the hard, woody ones, but the soft green ones are full of flavour – why waste them?).

Finely chop your lettuce or spring greens. When the pasta is cooked, remove from the heat. Before you drain it, toss the greens into the water to blanch them briefly. Drain, add the herbs and toss thoroughly.

Grate the cheese and scatter it over the top. Serve, with a knob of the butter on top and a good grinding of black pepper.

TIP: To make this extra special, add chilli and garlic, or bacon, or all three.

Birthday pizza sauce

In my household, there are two birthdays in March, mine and Small Boy's. We celebrated both this year with home-made pizza and cake. Cooking in our household is often a family affair – and on this occasion I was Sauce Chef. By my own admission, this is the ultimate pizza sauce, spooned generously on to home-made dough (see opposite) and topped with an assortment of things from the fridge. It doubled up as a pasta sauce the next day, too, ideal for post-birthday unwillingness to cook while nursing quite a headache . . .

Makes a very large jar

4 fat cloves of garlic or 6 smaller ones

1 onion

50g butter or 50ml oil, sunflower or groundnut

1 teaspoon fennel seeds

a fistful of flat-leaf parsley

1 tablespoon white wine vinegar

1 tablespoon sugar

2 x 400g tins of chopped tomatoes

2 tablespoons tomato purée

a generous pinch of salt

Peel and finely chop the garlic. Peel and slice the onion. Heat the butter or oil in a medium saucepan. Toss in the garlic, and onion with the fennel seeds and cook over a low heat for 6–8 minutes until the onions have started to soften – they don't need to be translucent as they'll carry on cooking in the sauce. Don't rush this – burned onions will permeate the flavour of the sauce and melodramatically ruin it. It's just a few minutes: stir. Chop the parsley, discarding any tough stalks.

Add the vinegar and cook for 1 minute until it loses its acrid vinegary smell, then add the sugar, tomatoes, tomato purée, salt and parsley.

Bring to a vigorous boil, allow it to spit and splutter for a minute or two, then reduce to a low heat. Give it a good stir to make sure it isn't sticking to the bottom of the pan, scrape the thickening layer from the edges, and leave to simmer for 20 minutes.

TIP: Add an extra 10–20 minutes to the cooking time for a richer, more decadent, more concentrated sauce, or allow to cool completely for a similar effect. Even better spooned into a jar and left in the fridge. Reheat as needed.

Birthday pizza dough

Makes a 30cm square pizza – a genius concept: square and rectangular pizzas fit baking trays and ovens far better than round ones

210g plain flour, plus extra for dusting

6g (1½ teaspoons) fast-action dried yeast

125ml hot water

1 tablespoon oil

1 teaspoon sugar

½ teaspoon salt

semolina for dusting (optional)

Originally from Allegra's *Big Table, Busy Kitchen*, this recipe has become Birthday Pizza in our house – we had it on my and Small Boy's birthday, a pizza-fest in March. I've adapted it for those who don't have food processors, because I'm a simple soul.

Preheat the oven to 220°C/425°F/gas 7.

Pour 70g of the flour into a bowl with the yeast and stir together slowly as you tip in the hot water. As soon as it's come together, add the oil, sugar, salt and remaining flour, and stir again until everything is combined. This should take less than a minute. Tip the dough on to a floured surface and knead until it's springy to touch.

Pop it into a floured bowl, cover with cling film and leave it for the yeast to activate, about 30 minutes.

Dust the bottom of your baking tray with semolina, if you have it, or flour if you haven't. Dust the work surface with flour and roll out the dough into a square 2–3mm thick.

Add the Birthday Pizza Sauce (see opposite), or a squidge of tomato purée and some herbs if you're feeling lazy, or whatever odds and ends you have in the fridge. The kids like ham, tomato and cheese, but I flung an aubergine and a courgette on mine, with some sliced mozzarella and chilli flakes.

Bake in the centre of the oven for 10–12 minutes, until the edges are golden and crispy. Serve and enjoy.

finished dish

olives

dough

ham

basil

mozzarella

sauce

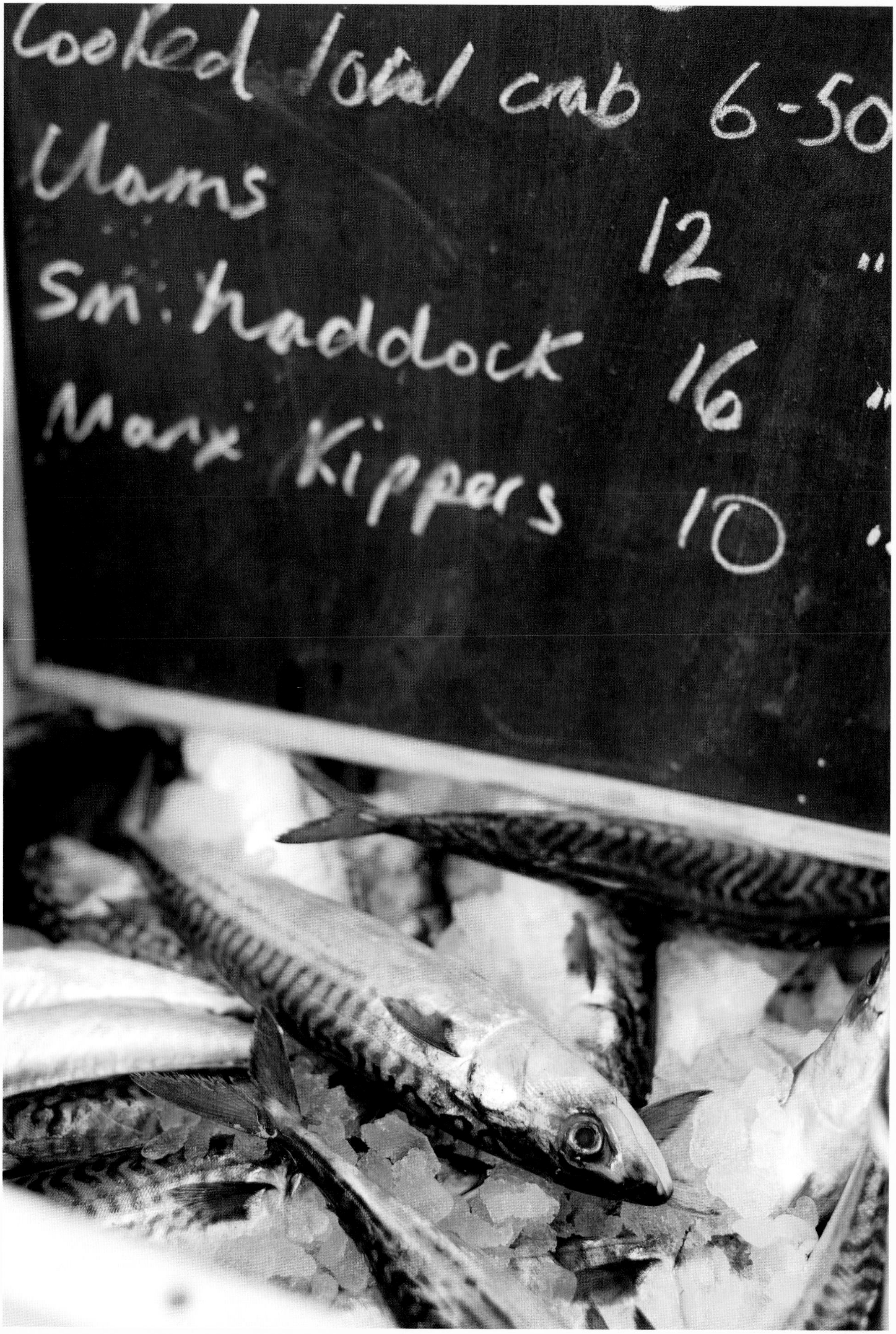
Cooked local crab 6-50
Clams 12
Sm: haddock 16
Manx Kippers 10

MAY | JUN

07

summer herbs | sardines | mackerel
spinach | radishes

May and June were celebratory months, with
this beautiful book being finished – after
many late nights propping myself up on my
elbow at the kitchen table, scribbling bits on
notebooks on trains and in my mobile phone
when I got an idea or two, it was finally put
together and photographed in the early-
summer sunshine. And as I sit on my front
doorstep typing this up, I think how much a
year can change things; from sleeping on a
mattress on a floor in a room I shared with
my son, to sitting in the summer sun typing
my second book, watching him play on his
scooter in the street – it's been up and down
a little bit, but it's definitely been a pretty
memorable year . . .

Tabbouleh-style rice

Traditionally, tabbouleh is made with bulghur wheat, but it's not something I use in anything else so I tend not to buy it. I adapted a traditional tabbouleh recipe to make a cold rice salad – delicious with brown or white rice. You can use bulghur wheat if you want to, or giant couscous is good too.

Serves 2

150g rice

½ cucumber

1 large beef tomato or 1 x 400g tin of chopped tomatoes, well drained

1 red onion

1 fat clove of garlic

zest and juice of 1 lemon or 2 tablespoons bottled lemon juice

2 tablespoons oil, sunflower or groundnut

a pinch of salt

a fistful of mint

a generous fistful of flat-leaf parsley

First bring a pan of water to the boil and add the rice. Reduce to a simmer and cook for 12–15 minutes until soft and tender. Drain, rinse thoroughly with cold water to cool, then leave to stand.

Meanwhile, dice the cucumber and the tomato. Peel and finely chop the onion and garlic. Put them all into a large bowl with the lemon zest and juice, the oil and salt. Finely chop the mint leaves and stir through. Chop the parsley, discarding any tough stalks.

Now add the cooled rice and toss everything together. Scatter over the parsley and toss again. Serve chilled or at room temperature.

Thai-style pesto-y stuff

This hot sticky good stuff came about, as usual, from a head in the fridge and some leftover scraps that were crying out to be used up. I started off with an idea for coriander pesto, then found some sad bits of ginger and some withered spring onions, and decided to take it in a Thai-paste direction instead. It worked, my goodness, it worked, and I made lots and came up with some clever uses for it, too.

Makes 2 small jars

4 fat cloves of garlic

a thumb of fresh ginger

4 spring onions or
1 small regular onion

1 fresh red chilli or a pinch
of dried chilli flakes

zest and juice of 1 lime or
lemon, or 2 tablespoons
of bottled lime or
lemon juice

a generous fistful of
coriander

2 rounded teaspoons
sugar

100g peanuts or
4 tablespoons peanut
butter

100ml oil, sunflower or
groundnut

Peel and finely slice the garlic and ginger – scrape the skin off the ginger with the side of a teaspoon so that you don't lose too much of the yummy root. Trim and remove the outer layer from the spring onions, then chop them, or peel and chop the onion. Slice the chilli, if using a fresh one.

Toss the garlic, ginger, spring onions or regular onion into a blender with the fresh chilli or the dried chilli flakes. Grate in the lime or lemon zest, then squeeze in the juice. Add the coriander, sugar, peanuts or peanut butter and the oil, then blitz until you have a rough, chunky paste. Spoon into clean jars and store in the fridge for 1 week or the freezer for up to 3 months.

TIPS: You can toss this mixture through pasta for a spicy snack or stir it through noodles and veg for a quick lunch or dinner. Use it as the base for a seriously interesting risotto, with an assortment of veg. Or as a base for soup, with coconut milk and – yep – vegetables. Plaster it over chicken or fish before you cook it. Use it as a curry paste, with a little natural yoghurt and, of course, veg! Or come up with some fabulous new use for it and drop me a line to let me know . . .

Sardine rillettes

I love rillettes. The first time I heard the word, I was having dinner at the cookery writer Xanthe Clay's house, and she produced rabbit rillettes. I gobbled half the jar, and still haven't got around to procuring the recipe from her. For the uninitiated, rillettes is a chunky rough pâté, served a little cooler than room temperature and best smeared on warm toast. I couldn't do Xanthe's rabbit rillettes justice in a reconstruction, so here's a sardine one, all of my own.

Serves 2

1 onion

2 x 100g tins of sardines packed in oil

a fistful of flat-leaf parsley

100g soft cream cheese

zest and juice of 1 lemon or 2 tablespoons bottled lemon juice

salt and pepper

First, peel and very finely dice the onion, then dice it some more, then dice it again. You want it minced, virtually undetectable, in teeny tiny pieces.

Remove the sardines from the cans, keeping the oil. Carefully open each one down the back and belly with a small sharp knife: remove the backbone and any large visible bones. Discard the bones, and put the sardines into a bowl. Chop the parsley, discarding any tough stalks.

Mash the sardines with a fork, then add the onion, half of the cream cheese and the parsley. Grate over the lemon zest, if using, squeeze in the juice, and mix well with a fork to form a rough paste. Add a little more cream cheese, then a little more, tasting as you go until you have a blend that pleases you – you may prefer less cream cheese than I use.

Season to taste. It can be served immediately, or chilled and brought to near room temperature to serve.

TIP: I like mine spread on hot toast, then dunked in tomato soup for a quick, lazy dinner.

Unapologetic puttanesca

Originally a 'slapper's supper' of store-cupboard ingredients, my recipe for puttanesca changes depending on what I have available in the kitchen. I prefer sardines to the more traditional anchovies, tipping in their oil for its distinctive flavour. This dish is a hot, fast joyride for your tastebuds – an enigmatic explosion of fiery chilli and soft fish, vinegary capers and a salty aftertaste. It's punchy and unapologetic. I cook my spaghetti in the sauce to save on washing up and in keeping with the 'fling it all in' ethos.

Serves 2

4 fat cloves of garlic

1 fresh red chilli or a generous pinch of dried chilli flakes

a knob of butter

1 x 400g tin of chopped tomatoes

1 x 100g tin of sardines

150g spaghetti

1 rounded tablespoon olives

1 rounded tablespoon capers

salt and pepper

Peel the garlic and roughly chop it – I like mine fat and chunky in a dish like this, but if the thought of a mouthful of slightly crunchy, tangy garlic terrifies you, chop it finely. Slice the fresh chilli, if using. Toss the garlic and chilli, fresh or dried flakes, into a large saucepan with the butter, and cook over a low heat for a few minutes until they have softened.

Pour over the chopped tomatoes and the oil from the sardines, with a splash of water, and crank up the heat to bring it to the boil. Feed the spaghetti into the hot sauce as it boils, then reduce to a simmer, stirring gently.

Meanwhile, carefully remove the bones from the sardines by splitting them, belly and back, with a small sharp knife. Use the tip of the knife to pick out the large bone in the middle, and any visible ones. Break the sardines into chunks and stir into the sauce. Dice the olives.

When the spaghetti has softened and the sauce thickened, divide between two bowls and top with the capers, olives, a pinch of salt and a grinding of pepper. Eat!

Smoked mackerel kedgeree

The mackerel can be replaced with any smoked or strongly flavoured fish, and you can swap the spices for garam masala or curry powder, whatever you have to hand. The onions lend a soft sweetness, the rice fills you up, and the little chunks of egg and mackerel are groan-inducingly gorgeous. Try it.

Serves 2

1 onion

1 tablespoon oil, sunflower or groundnut

1 teaspoon turmeric

1 teaspoon ground cumin

150g rice

1 egg, or 2, if you like

150g smoked mackerel

50g frozen spinach

salt and pepper

Peel and finely slice the onion. Heat the oil in a pan, add the onion and cook for 8–10 minutes over a medium heat until it has softened. Add the spices and stir for another minute.

Put in the rice with enough water to cover, and stir. Cover the pan and cook for 15 minutes, until the rice is soft and swollen. Take it off the heat.

Meanwhile, boil a separate small saucepan of water, and pop in the egg(s). Simmer for 10 minutes to hard-boil, then plunge into cold water to cool.

Flake the mackerel with a fork, discarding the skin, and add it to the pan with the spinach. Reheat until the spinach has defrosted and is hot. Taste, and season. Peel the egg(s) and cut into chunks, then scatter over the finished dish.

Serve with fresh parsley or coriander to garnish, if you have it.

Smoked mackerel, chilli and lemon fishcakes

Smoked mackerel gives these fishcakes an intense flavour, but for a cheaper version, tinned sardines work well with the chilli and lemon. I quarter my mixture and make 4 quite substantial fishcakes, but this quantity will do 6–8 quite easily.

Makes 4 large fishcakes

500g potatoes
a fistful of flat-leaf parsley
1 tablespoon lemon juice
½ teaspoon dried chilli flakes
300g smoked mackerel
1 rounded tablespoon flour, plus extra for dusting
2 tablespoons oil

Peel and dice the potatoes, then put them into a saucepan of boiling water, reduce the heat and simmer until tender, for about 15 minutes. Chop the parsley, discarding any tough stalks.

Drain and mash the potatoes with the parsley, lemon juice and chilli flakes. Flake the fish into the mash, add the flour and mix well. With floured hands, shape into fishcakes.

Put them on a plate and chill in the fridge for at least 30 minutes (or freeze for future use).

When the fishcakes are cold, fry them in the oil over a medium heat for 7 minutes on each side.

Serve with green vegetables and tartare sauce.

Chickpeas with spinach and cumin

I make these chickpeas two ways, depending on how healthy or naughty I'm feeling. First up is this recipe, cooked lightly with spinach, garlic and cumin for a simple side dish or to toss through a salad. Sometimes, when I need a treat or something to pick at, I deep-fry the lot, let it cool, tip it into a bowl and snack away.

Serves 2 as a main dish or several as a side

1 onion

2 fat cloves of garlic

1 fresh chilli or a pinch of dried chilli flakes

2 tablespoons oil, sunflower or groundnut

1 teaspoon ground cumin

1 x 400g tin of chickpeas

200g fresh or frozen spinach, defrosted

salt and pepper

a generous squeeze of lemon juice

Peel and finely slice the onion and garlic. Slice the fresh chilli, if using. Heat the oil in a frying pan and toss in all three with the cumin. Cook over a low heat for 8–10 minutes, or until the onions have softened.

Drain and rinse the chickpeas, then add to the pan with the spinach and stir through. Crank up the heat to wilt the spinach and lightly fry the chickpeas, stirring to stop them sticking to the pan.

Season, then serve with the lemon juice.

Spinach and lentil daal

This recipe started life as a 'use-up dinner' for leftovers from a *Guardian* shoot – I'd made my Beetroot, Feta Cheese and Lentil Salad (see page 16) and had a pile of lentils and half a bag of spinach left. It quickly became one of my favourite go-to recipes for a quick and simple supper – ideal for evenings eating on my own, or when I don't really fancy cooking beyond chucking some stuff into a pot and flopping down at the table. We all have nights like that and here's a solution for yours. For an even better store-cupboard version, keep some frozen spinach handy and eat it straight from the pan. Bish, bash, bosh, done.

Serves 2

1 onion

1 fresh red chilli or a pinch of dried chilli flakes

1 tablespoon oil, sunflower or groundnut

2 teaspoons ground cumin or turmeric, or 1 teaspoon of each, if you have them

1 chicken stock cube

100g red split lentils

200ml water

130g spinach, fresh or frozen

fresh coriander or parsley or mint (optional)

200ml natural yoghurt

1 tablespoon lemon juice

Peel and finely slice the onion. Finely chop the fresh chilli, if using. Heat the oil in a large frying pan, then add the onion, chilli, fresh or dried flakes, spices and crumbled stock cube. Cook over a gentle heat for 10 minutes, until the onions have softened.

Thoroughly rinse the lentils and add them to the pan. Turn up the heat to medium, and stir. Let them toast for a few minutes, then add half of the water. Stir in quickly – it will absorb quite fast.

Chop the spinach and add to the pan (if using frozen spinach just put it straight in, breaking it up with a wooden spoon as it starts to thaw). Add the remaining water and stir through, then continue cooking for about 10 minutes, until the lentils are ready. Chop the fresh herb, if using, discarding any tough stalks.

Stir in the yoghurt and the lemon juice. Serve with a fresh herb if you have one to hand.

TIP: Leftovers can be thinned with a little stock to make a delicious soup, or tossed through pasta. It will keep in the fridge for 2 days, or you can freeze it in an ice-cube tray for easy portions.

Pearl barley risotto

This recipe doesn't involve the characteristic standing-and-stirring of a risotto, so I'm not really sure what to call it, apart from bloody yummy – I'm tucking into it as I type this! I haven't overloaded it with too many flavours, as the chewy nuttiness of pearl barley speaks for itself, but it would be delicious as a side dish with juicy chicken, or padded out as a cold salad with sliced black olives and tomatoes – a sort of tabbouleh, if you will.

Serves 2

3 cups of water

1 cup of chicken stock

juice of 1 lemon or
2 tablespoons bottled
lemon juice

160g pearl barley

100g fresh or frozen
spinach, defrosted

50g feta cheese

Pour the water, stock and 1 tablespoon of the lemon juice into a large saucepan and add the pearl barley. Bring to the boil, and boil vigorously for 10 minutes, then reduce the heat and simmer until the pearl barley is tender, for about 20 minutes. If it seems to be drying out, add a little more water.

Add the spinach to the pan, stir it through and let it warm for 5 minutes. Chop the parsley, discarding any tough stalks.

To serve, crumble the cheese and scatter it across the top with the parsley, then squeeze or drizzle over the remaining lemon juice.

Delicious hot or cold.

TIP: It would benefit from a drizzle of oil when served – like the Spanish do with a good paella. Add chopped parsley if you have it handy.

Spinach, lentil and lemon soup

This easy, comforting spinach and lentil soup was inspired by a recipe in *Saha*, by Greg and Lucy Malouf. I made it a few times as a quick late-night supper, before I lost the Moleskine notebook with the details in one of my many house moves. Here's what I remember of it, with a few blanks filled in.

Serves 2

1 onion

1 fat clove of garlic or 2 smaller ones

1 tablespoon oil, sunflower or groundnut

150g lentils

1 litre stock

zest and juice of 2 lemons or 4 tablespoons bottled lemon juice

a mugful of fresh or frozen spinach, defrosted

a fistful of coriander

pine nuts (optional)

Peel and chop the onion and garlic. Heat the oil in a saucepan and cook them until they are soft, for 8–10 minutes. Rinse the lentils and tip them into the pan, followed by the stock, then stir. Bring it to the boil, reduce the heat and simmer for 30 minutes. Grate the zest from the lemons, if using, and squeeze out the juice. Roughly chop the spinach and coriander. Stir the lemon zest and juice, the spinach and coriander into the soup. Whiz everything together with a blender or in a food processor. Scatter over some pine nuts if you're feeling fancy!

Radish tops and garlic cream pizza

Last spring I had a delicious nettle and garlic pizza, devoured it, enjoyed it, and promptly forgot about it . . . until I had a glut of radish tops to use up from my enthusiastic radish-growing adventure a few months later. Radish tops and nettles taste quite similar, so I've recreated the delicious pizza with my glut of green leaves and lashings of smashed-up garlic softened in a luxurious cream base . . .

Makes 1 pizza

2 fat cloves of garlic

a knob of butter

a splash of water

70ml white wine

100ml double cream

salt and pepper

a fistful of radish tops

2 tablespoons oil

1 pizza base – see Birthday Pizza Dough recipe on page 209, or buy one ready made

2 balls of mozzarella, sliced

a fistful of hard, strong cheese

Smash and chop the garlic and toss into a saucepan with the butter and a splash of water. Cook on a very low heat for a few minutes, until the butter has melted and the garlic starts to soften. Pour in the wine, keeping the heat low, for an extra four minutes. Add the cream and stir in, season well, and simmer until reduced by half, for approximately five minutes.

Meanwhile, roughly chop the radish greens – large ones may have a mild sting, as the underside of the leaves can be rough and scratchy, so handle with care. They lose their sting once cooked, just like nettles! If they do nip you, rinse your hands under the cold tap for half a minute to soothe them. Pop the greens into a mixing bowl and toss with oil and salt and pepper.

Spread the garlicky cream on to the pizza base, top with the sliced mozzarella and greens, and grate hard, strong cheese over the top. Bake in the centre of the oven at 180°C/350°F/gas 4 for 12 minutes, or until the cheese is melted and golden, and the pizza is crisp round the edges. Then enjoy!

Radish top pesto

You know me, I love a pesto as a useful receptacle for all things green – and the peppery tops of my radishes are no exception. Radish tops don't stay fresh for very long, so once separated from the little pink or purple radishes, bag them up or wrap them in slightly damp paper, store in the fridge, and eat within a day or two. The taste is something like nettles, but milder, and can be tossed into salads or wilted into curries. The larger leaves can be rough and stingy to touch, so not recommended for salads, but can be made into great pesto instead . . .

Makes 1 jar

2 fat cloves of garlic

a fistful or two of radish leaves

30g hard, strong cheese

50ml oil – sunflower, groundnut or olive oil

zest and juice of half a lemon

50g cashew nuts or pine nuts

Finely chop the garlic and leaves, and grate the cheese. Place in a blender with the oil, lemon juice and nuts, and pulse until smooth.

TIP: Store in a clean jar in the fridge for up to 1 week, or in the freezer for up to 3 months.

Radish and pea risotto

This year, we grew 'family radishes' at home on the roof, popping some seeds in compost and earth in a sunny spot, and pulling up a hundred radishes a few weeks later. Radishes are easy to grow, with a fast turnaround that makes them suitable for young children who might lose interest in the long months it takes to sprout a garlic bulb, or grow a carrot! Having a hundred radishes at our disposal meant I had to find ways to use them up ... As ever, when I start with a new ingredient, I showcase it in a risotto while I work out what to do with it, and this bright fresh summery version didn't disappoint!

Serves 4

1 large onion

2 fat cloves of garlic

a knob of butter

400g long grain rice

150ml white wine

1 litre chicken stock

200g radishes

a fistful of hard, strong cheese

a fistful of mint or parsley

150g peas

juice of half a lemon or 2 tablespoons bottled lemon juice

Finely slice the onion and chop the garlic, and toss into your pan with the butter on a low heat. Cook for 10 minutes, stirring occasionally to prevent the onions sticking to the pan.

When the onion and garlic have softened, add the rice and bring the heat up to medium. Cook for a few minutes until the edges of the rice are translucent.

Pour over the wine and stir. When the wine is almost all absorbed, add a large splash of stock, stir again, and repeat, until the rice is al dente or cooked to your liking – this may not use all of the stock, or you may need to add a splash of water if you like your risotto soupy and creamy.

While the rice is cooking, wash and slice your radishes in halves or quarters, grate your cheese, and finely chop the mint or parsley.

When the rice is al dente, toss in the radishes and peas, and stir again to combine. Cook for a further 5 minutes to warm the vegetables through and defrost the peas, if using frozen ones.

Serve topped with the chopped parsley or mint, the grated cheese and the lemon juice.

YEAR-ROUND COMFORTS

08

peanut butter | flour | oats
onions | bananas

Some of my favourite recipes use ingredients that are easy to buy all year round, like peanut butter, oats, onions and bananas. When I started writing this book, I was reluctant to include this chapter, as I felt it was a bit of a cop-out in a seasonal recipe book, but John, who heads up the design team at Penguin, remarked that inexperienced or not very confident cooks might find this chapter a good place to start – with store-cupboard ingredients and simple recipes – and I agreed! Besides, some of these are such favourites, it would have been a shame not to include them. Peanut Butter Hot Chocolate (page 247) takes just a few minutes, and has many dedicated fans on my blog and places like Instagram, where I get sent photo after photo of delicious-looking thick hot chocolate in a varity of gorgeous big mugs. The Bannocks (page 254) were a recipe from my *Guardian* column, and sustained me through my Live Below the Line challenge this year – made simply with oats and water – and the Make-Me-Better Morning Mug (page 247) is a must for banishing that heavy winter head feeling . . .

Peanut butter semi-freddo

Hot on the heels of my peanut butter frozen yoghurt recipe from my first book comes a peanut butter semi-freddo – gorgeously decadent on its own, or with the Maple Syrup Sponge Cake on page 248 for an American twist. Sometimes I sprinkle this with smashed-up crispy bacon – trust me and try it.

Serves 6

4 egg yolks
160g caster sugar
400ml double cream
220g peanut butter
2 tablespoons peanuts, salted or unsalted

Beat the egg yolks until pale and creamy, then pour in the sugar, cream and peanut butter. Beat well until thick and forming stiff peaks, and the peanut butter is evenly distributed.

Line a loaf tin with 2 layers of cling film, leaving a few centimetres hanging over the edges to fold over the top. Finely chop and smash the peanuts and scatter over the bottom of the tin. Pour in the semi-freddo mixture, and smooth the surface with a spoon.

Gently fold the cling film over the top and pop into the freezer for at least 4 hours.

Remove from the freezer for 5 minutes to soften before serving.

Peanut butter bread

I'm a massive fan of the humble peanut butter – almost obsessive, in fact. I've smuggled it into a sauce for chicken, celebrated it in a frozen yoghurt, and paired it with jam for cutesy thumbprint cookies. Now it's peanut butter bread. A favourite in my household, it's great toasted with butter or jam, dunked into soups, or eaten warm and cakey with a dollop of custard . . .

Serves 4

60g butter, plus a little extra for greasing

300g flour

1 tablespoon baking powder

120g sugar – brown is best but white is fine

150g peanut butter

250ml milk

1 egg

Preheat the oven to 180°C/350°F/gas 4. Lightly grease a loaf tin, and set to one side.

Tip the flour into a large bowl and add the baking powder and sugar. Stir briefly to combine.

Pop the butter and peanut butter into a small saucepan over a low heat and stir to soften. (Or put them into a dish and stick them in the microwave for 1 minute on a high heat, then stir well to soften.)

Make a well in the centre of the dry ingredients. Tip in the melted peanut butter mix and the milk. Break in the egg, and stir well until combined.

Pour the batter into the loaf tin and bake for 50 minutes, until risen and golden brown, and a knife inserted into the centre comes out clean.

Allow to cool before serving.

Peanut butter hot chocolate

Sometimes I make things I love so much that I wonder how I'll ever bring myself to eat anything else. This is one of those things that brings silent moments of appreciative bliss when I go all *When Harry Met Sally* about food. Although this time, it's a drink.

Makes 1 mug

50ml water

3 squares of milk or dark chocolate

1 heaped tablespoon smooth peanut butter

150ml milk

This is really simple. Pop the water, chocolate and peanut butter into a small saucepan on a medium heat. Stir well until the chocolate and peanut butter have melted and form a glossy, sticky paste. Add a splash of the milk and stir in, repeat with a bigger splash, then the rest. Don't put it all in at once – it'll be hard to get the lumps out!

Pour into your favourite mug, sit, sip and forget about everything else.

TIP: You can use milk powder and 150ml water to make up the milk for this.

Make-me-better morning mug

Scratchy throat, simultaneous blocked and runny nose, muggy head, general air of malaise? Yeah, that was me, one desperate husky, groggy morning in January (and February and March). In a bid to banish the heavy-cold feeling, I knocked up a large jug of this stuff – and, by golly, it worked a treat. If you have an office job, take it to work in a Thermos flask or similar, and sip it at your desk to banish the blues. Or take the day off, curl up with a book and snooze, sip, snooze, sip . . .

Makes a 1 litre jug – drink the lot!

1 litre water

1 lemon

a thumb of fresh ginger

scant ½ teaspoon turmeric

2 tablespoons runny honey

Boil 1 litre of water. Quarter and dice the lemon and toss into the bottom of the jug. Finely chop 1cm of the ginger and add, with the turmeric and honey. Pour over half of the water and stir well, then top up with the rest. Strain into a mug and drink.

I kept topping mine up with boiling water, adding extra turmeric and honey, all day. I felt much better for it!

Maple syrup sponge cake

This sweet, sticky cake came about by accident while we were shooting the photography for this book – I fancied cake to keep me going through the long days, and this is what happened. If you don't keep maple syrup in the house, you obviously don't have as much of a pancake habit as we do, and you can use golden syrup or treacle instead. If you like, you can use half caster sugar and half demerara for a deep treacly sweetness.

Serves 4

110g butter
220g maple syrup
125g caster sugar
125g self-raising flour
1 large egg
150ml milk

Preheat the oven to 140°C/275°F/gas 1.

Pop the butter into a small saucepan with the maple syrup and place over a low heat, stirring occasionally to melt and combine.

In a large mixing bowl, stir together the sugar and flour. Break in the egg, pour over the milk and mix together with a wooden spoon. Pour over the melted butter and syrup, and stir well to form a smooth runny batter.

Lightly grease a cake tin, and pour in the batter. Bake in the centre of the oven for 30 minutes, then turn the heat up to 180°C/350°F/gas 4 for a further 20 minutes.

Serve warm – it doesn't need any accompaniment, but if you fancy a real treat, serve it with the Peanut Butter Semifreddo on page 242.

TIP: They will keep in an airtight container for 3 days. Alternatively open-freeze them on a baking sheet, then put them into freezer bags. Bake them from frozen for 15–18 minutes.

Iced breakfast tarts

As a child I loved Pop-Tarts™, those saccharine toaster pastries thick with white icing and multicoloured sprinkles that, when eaten greedily from the toaster, would scald your tongue with red-hot jam. I decided to see if I could make my own version from scratch, pastry and all, and here they are. They're not an everyday breakfast but they're definitely a why-the-hell-not breakfast!

Makes 8

100g unsalted butter, plus extra for greasing

200g flour, plus extra for the worktop

6 tablespoons cold water

6–8 tablespoons jam, raspberry or strawberry

6 tablespoons icing sugar, approx. 60g

sprinkles

Preheat the oven to 180°C/350°F/gas 4.

First, make the pastry. Either melt the butter in a bowl in the microwave and mix it quickly into the flour to form a breadcrumb mixture – but this will need to go into the fridge for at least an hour to bring it down to a workable temperature – or cube the butter and rub it into the flour with your fingertips to form a fine breadcrumb consistency. This won't need to be chilled as you haven't heated the butter. Add 1 tablespoon of water at a time, then mix with a knife until it just forms a dough.

Flour your worktop and tip out the dough. Now halve it, so you have a manageable amount to work with, and roll it out very thinly, 2–3mm thick. I don't have a rolling pin so used a lemon-juice bottle, floured – as the song almost went, Any Bottle Will Do.

When the pastry is rolled out, cut into 16 rectangles about 10cm x 7cm each. That's a guess, by the way. Slightly bigger or slightly smaller is just fine (in fact, I want to make mini ones). Get as many rectangles as you can from your pastry, adding the cut-offs back to the rest on the side and re-rolling as necessary.

Spread jam thinly on half of the rectangles, leaving a generous 1–2cm space around the edges. Place a plain rectangle on top of a jammy one, and press together lightly. Trim the edges with a sharp knife to neaten.

Grease a baking sheet and place the tarts on it very carefully.

Repeat these steps until all of the pastry dough is used up, making 8 in total.

Bake in the centre of the oven for 14–16 minutes until lightly golden. Remove from the oven and leave to cool for half an hour. Don't worry if they feel slightly soft: they'll harden as they cool.

Make up the icing: mix the icing sugar with 1 tablespoon of the water in a small bowl, and spread on top of the cooled tart. Add sprinkles immediately, while the icing is still soft, and leave to set.

They can be eaten cold, or warmed gently in the oven.

Super-express portable porridge

I first came up with this not-really-a-recipe as a solution to overpriced porridge sachets for a friend of mine – and subsequently revolutionized her morning routine and her wallet. I like mine with sultanas, for juicy, bursting goodness, but have a play around with it. It's also good with chunks of chocolate, or honey, or any fresh or dried fruit.

Makes around 20 adult portions, or 30 child-sized

1kg porridge oats
400g dried milk powder
250g sultanas
100g sugar

Pour all of the ingredients into a large airtight container and close the lid tightly. Shake well to distribute.

Find a cup or container that measures out your perfect porridge portion – less is more: remember, that stuff grows! Mine is a 90ml espresso cup, roughly equal to 3 rounded tablespoons.

Add twice as much volume of cold water to the porridge mix, loosely cover the container or bowl, and microwave on full power for 1 minute. Remove, stir, add a splash more water if necessary (not all oats are created equal), and microwave for another minute.

Remove from the microwave, stir again, and leave to stand for a minute before tucking in.

TIP: If you don't have a microwave handy – in my experience, some workplaces are far better equipped than others – then pour boiled water over, cover, leave to stand for a few minutes to soak, then stir and eat.

Peanut butter granola

I made this first for myself as I love peanut butter in the mornings. Making toast under the grill inevitably goes wrong when you have a three-year-old to get washed, socked and shod in the mornings, so I cobbled this together and bunged it in a big jar. Perfect with hot or cold milk, or pop it into the microwave for 60 seconds and have a warm, soft, stodgy, comforting start to your day.

There are endless variations to this. Try all butter instead of the peanut butter to hold your oats together (ooo-er), and dark chocolate, with toasted or ground almonds, if the purse stretches. White chocolate is good for the sweet-of-tooth, while milk chocolate and marmalade, in place of the honey, taste similar to a famous round chocolate orange in a bright blue box. If you feel like erring on the side of virtue, chop a banana into it.

Makes 8 portions

25g butter, plus a little extra for greasing

4 tablespoons peanut butter

4 tablespoons honey

300g rolled porridge oats

Preheat the oven to 180°C/350°F/gas 4. Lightly grease a baking tray.

Melt the butter, peanut butter and honey together – either in a medium saucepan on a low heat for a minute or two, or in the microwave on full power for 30 seconds – and stir to combine.

Add the oats and mix well.

Tip the granola on to the baking tray, flattening it down with the back of a spoon to spread approximately 1cm thick. Bake in the centre of the oven for 15 minutes.

Remove and allow to cool for a further 15 minutes before transferring to an airtight container.

Bannocks

There are easily a hundred variations on the humble oatcake, and it took me six attempts to nail this one. These hearty, knobbly little things were exactly what I had in mind when I set out to make something to smear some soft cheese and jam on for a mid-afternoon snack. Make them fatter, thinner, bigger, smaller – leave half of the oats whole if you wish. Smear them with butter and/or jam, pile them with cheese, pop them into the kids' lunchboxes or sneak a couple into your work bag. Now I've worked out how to make them with ingredients I always have in the house, I'm never more than a few minutes away from a pile of bannocks. Huzzah!

Makes 12

30g butter, plus a little extra for greasing

a splash of water

120g oats

a pinch of salt

flour, for dusting

Preheat the oven to 180°C/350°F/gas 4.

Pop the butter into a small saucepan with the water over a medium heat, to melt the butter and warm the water.

Pour the oats into a blender and blast until they're mostly ground down – a few left whole add a crunchy texture, but don't fret about it too much. Tip into the saucepan with the salt and stir to form a sticky dough. Leave to cool, covered, for 30 minutes.

Dust a work surface with flour, and pat the dough out to flatten and shape. I use my hands for this, to press the oats together, slapping it gently with my palms and fingertips until it's around 5mm thick. Use a cookie cutter or the top of a mug to cut into circles – as large or as small as you like.

Grease a baking tray. Lay the bannocks on it and put it into the oven for 20 minutes, turning them halfway through. Allow to cool and harden before eating.

Cheese and onion drop scones

Drop scones first made their way into my repertoire as a finger food for my son, because they are soft and easy for his little hands and mouth. As he's grown older – and now has all his own teeth – I've added different things to the basic recipe. They're great with a fried or poached egg, a couple of sausages, or simply dunked in ketchup.

Serves 2

½ onion

30g hard, strong cheese

2 sprigs of parsley

100g flour

1 egg

100ml milk

4 tablespoons oil, sunflower or groundnut

Peel and very finely chop the onion. Grate the cheese and chop the parsley, discarding any tough stalks. Put them all into a mixing bowl.

Add the flour, and stir to distribute the dry ingredients evenly. Make a well in the centre and break in the egg. Pour over the milk, and beat briskly with a fork to form a smooth batter.

Heat the oil in a frying pan. When it is smoking hot, drop in a tablespoon of batter. Fry over a medium heat for 30 seconds on each side, then remove to a plate lined with kitchen paper to soak up any excess oil, and keep warm. Repeat until all of the batter is used.

TIP: Delicious eaten on their own, but I had mine with an egg and a cup of coffee – well, it was nearly lunchtime!

Blue cheese and onion tattie scones

These simple but hearty scones are ideal for any time of day. I serve mine for breakfast with a runny egg on top, or for dinner with buttery cabbage and succulent chicken thighs.

Serves 4

500g potatoes

1 onion

1 egg

a few sprigs of thyme or parsley

25g butter, plus extra for greasing

50g blue cheese

150g flour, plus extra for the worktop

salt and pepper

oil, sunflower or groundnut, for frying

Boil a medium pan of water. Peel and dice the potatoes, add them to the pan and simmer until they're very soft, 10–12 minutes.

Peel and finely chop the onion. Beat the egg and pick 2 teaspoons of leaves from the thyme sprigs or parsley. Drain and mash the potatoes with the butter and onion. Allow to cool slightly, then mix in the egg with the crumbled cheese and thyme or parsley leaves. Stir in the flour for a stiff mixture to form the scones, adding a touch extra, if necessary. Season generously with salt and pepper.

Dust your worktop with flour, and roll out the dough in a rough 16cm circle, 1cm thick – I don't own a rolling pin so I use a bottle, floured. For the traditional wedge shapes, cut the circle into 6 wedges.

Heat a little oil in a large frying pan and fry the wedges over a medium to low heat (in batches if necessary), for 4–5 minutes on each side, until golden brown and crisp.

For a healthier option, bake on a greased baking tray in the oven at 180°C/350°F/gas 4 for 20–25 minutes, until golden brown, turning over halfway through the cooking time.

Allow to cool and firm up slightly before serving.

TIP: Greek-style cheese and chopped spinach are a delicious combination that works brilliantly in these scones. They're perfect with a grilled tomato or two on top for breakfast or lunch.

Sticky salted banana loaf cake

This soft, sticky banana cake is nicknamed 'Fairtrade Cake' in my notebook, as it uses Fairtrade bananas and sugar, and peanuts when I have them. The caramel sauce isn't essential – leave it out for kids' lunchboxes – but it does add a seriously special twist for a dessert.

Serves 4–6

100g butter, softened

200g sugar

4 eggs

200g natural yoghurt

2 bananas

200g flour

1 teaspoon bicarbonate of soda

scant ½ teaspoon ground cinnamon

a pinch of salt

For the sauce:

100g sugar

Preheat the oven to 140°C/275°F/gas 1.

Beat together the butter and sugar, and mix in the eggs and yoghurt. Peel and break up the bananas and mash them in with a fork or wooden spoon. Stir well to combine.

Tip in the flour, add the bicarb, cinnamon and salt, and mix well.

Transfer to a loaf tin and bake in the centre of the oven for 45 minutes to 1 hour, until a knife inserted into the middle comes out clean.

Meanwhile, make the caramel sauce. Pour the sugar into a heavy-bottomed saucepan over a medium heat and leave it for a few minutes. As it starts to soften and melt at the edges, stir it in and leave it for a few more minutes. The change happens quickly – one minute you have a pile of sugar that looks like it isn't doing anything, and the next you have a soft, silky caramel sauce. Remove from the heat and add a splash of cold water (it will hiss and bubble a little, so don't get too close), stirring in quickly. Return to a low heat to keep it soft and warm while the cake cooks.

Serve the cake with caramel sauce dribbled over the top.

TIP: Sprinkle 2 tablespoons of chopped salted peanuts over the caramel sauce.

Sterilizing jars

The only exception to sterilizing jars is when I'm popping some leftover pasta sauce in one to put in the fridge to use in the week, or a bit of pesto, etc. – I just pop it into a clean dry jar with a good-fitting lid. I keep a drawer full of jars in the kitchen, washed and recycled from jams, pickles, mayonnaise, mustard, peanut butter and tiny little spice jars, all of which come in very handy in our busy kitchen. If I've made a batch of jam or marmalade, or something that has taken lots of time and love, the last thing I want is to pop it into a dirty jar and be throwing it away a few weeks later. Sterilizing jars is quick and easy – here's a few methods that I use.

Oven:

Heat the oven to 120°C – no higher, or you run the risk of the glass shattering, and an oven full of glass is not the most fun thing in the world to clean, not to mention slightly hazardous! Pop your jars on a baking sheet, or if you don't have a baking sheet, a double layer of newspaper on each oven shelf (but not the bottom of the oven) works just as well. Lay the jars on their sides on the shelves with the lids off, not touching each other, and close the oven door. Bake your jars for 20 minutes, and remove carefully with a double-folded tea-towel or thick oven glove. Fill your hot jars with hot jam, before allowing them to cool – hot jam in cold jars means broken jars and a big mess.

Dishwasher:

If you have a dishwasher, pop them in on a quick hot setting – try to time it so your jars are clean when your jam/marmalade is ready to set.

Milton Sterilizing Fluid:

One for all the parents out there with half a bottle of sterilizing fluid stashed under the sink from days gone by! Simply fill up your sink or a bucket with cold water, add a capful of sterilizing fluid, pop your jars and lids in and leave them for 10 minutes. Remove, place top down on a clean tea- towel to drain, and fill with jam or other goodness.

Microwave:

Clean and thoroughly rinse your jars, leaving them wet. Pop them in the microwave for 30 seconds, a few at a time, to sterilize. Fill them while hot, and allow the jar and contents to cool together.

Index

Acknowledgements

First, thank you, you great person holding a copy of my book in your hands, for supporting me in my culinary and writing adventure.

To Adrian and Charlotte, for your support, guidance and kindness, as ever.

To Tamsin, Emma and Emily for patience; to Katya and Francesca for dealing with all the press enquiries on my behalf; to John for beautiful design work, and bringing some of my mad dreams to life. To Rob, for help cooking and shooting dishes, and Susan, for beautiful photos.

To Xanthe, for continuing to be a great friend and support, thank you. To Ros, for being there when I needed an ear to bend or a petition to wield, thank you. To Juliet and Jim, for letting me take over your house for Charity Curry Nights. To Sarah, for always being there when I need a good friend.

To Suse, for patience, guidance and encouragement, for taking my concept and fashioning it into a column in the *Guardian*, and for helping me grow.

To the Food Tube team, for taking me under your wing and into the family, and opening so many great doors — loved working with you guys and look forward to collaborating some more!

To the Sainsbury's team: thank you for the opportunity to work together. It was a mad experience but I loved it, and thank you so much.

To my readers, Twitter followers and Facebook fans, for being there with love, support and kind words day after day – thank you.

To Rosemary, Joanna and Aoife at United Agents – my knight(esses) in shining armour – to the future, and thank you.

To Tom and Megan at Blackfoot for always being so welcoming. To Matt and Rad for all the Salty Dogs and Moscow Mules consumed in the creation of this book. To Inma, Sarah and Hannah for giggles and great service. To Rory, James and Rob for all the pork.

To Lea, for all your help with the smallests while I got this thing written, and to Floss and DanDan for being such good friends in my new surroundings – thank you and love.

To Jonny and Delilah, for making me smile, for cuddles and kisses and sweetness, and for reminding me what's really important in this life and madness.

And, last, Allegra, for putting up with me crabby and angsty and bashing a book out in the very early days, for your love, your experience, your support, your kindness, your strength, for you. Not a hand-scrawled and smudged dedication this time. Thank you for making this my pretty good year.

Jack xxx